Or is that just Me?

RICHARD HAMMOND

PHOENIX

A PHOENIX PAPERBACK

First published in Great Britain in 2009
by Weidenfeld & Nicolson
This paperback edition published in 2010
by Phoenix,
an imprint of Orion Books Ltd,
Orion House, 5 Upper St Martin's Lane,
London WC2H 9EA

An Hachette UK company

1 3 5 7 9 10 8 6 4 2

A CIP catalogue record for this book
is available from the British Library.

ISBN 978-0-7538-2563-1

Printed and bound in Great Britain by Clays Ltd, St Ives plc

The Orion Publishing Group's policy is to use papers that
are natural, renewable and recyclable products and
made from wood grown in sustainable forests. The logging
and manufacturing processes are expected to conform to
the environmental regulations of the country of origin.

www.orionbooks.co.uk

Richard Ha[...] [...]esen-
ter whose wry and infectious humour first propelled him
to fame in 2002 as one third of the team on BBC2's flagship
programme, the world-conquering *Top Gear*, now in its
fourteenth series. He presented five seasons of *Brainiac*
Sky One, he was a regular team captain on the quiz show
Petrolheads and his *Richard Hammond's 5 O'Clock Show* was
shown every weekday on ITV1 for several months in
2006. Richard has also hosted his own bank holiday shows
on Radio 2.

He has made a number of TV documentaries, including
Richard Hammond Meets Evel Knievel, and in 2007 and 2009
he filmed the highly acclaimed National Geographic series
Engineering Connections. In early 2009 Richard presented
two new series for the BBC: *Blast Lab*, a BBC2 science
programme appealing to young children and the first series
that he both presented and co-developed with his own
production company, Hamster's Wheel; and the very popular *Total Wipeout* on BBC1.

Richard has also written a number of very successful
books, including *On The Edge*, in 2007, an account of his
near-fatal crash while filming for *Top Gear*, which was the
number one non-fiction hardback bestseller of the year.
The following year *As You Do*, his humorous look at the
year following his crash, also topped the bestseller lists.

By Richard Hammond

What Not to Drive
Car Confidential
On the Edge: My Story
As You Do
A Short History of Caravans in the UK
Or is that just Me?

To Mindy, Izzy and Willow.

Thanks to every member of all the film crews I have annoyed across the world. And to the crew of *HMS Illustrious* for making me welcome, showing me their amazing workplace and helping me see in my forties like a big, drunken dope. Thanks also to Mindy and the girls for allowing me to continue my inept wanderings across the globe. It's worth going away only because I get to come home to you.

Contents

List of Illustrations

a pig in salt. [1(Left, top & bottom), 3(right, top & bottom)]

Another box ticked – a world tour before the age of 40. With Jeremy and Steve Pizzati in Sydney. [4]

A helicopter pre-crash. It looked much the same post crash but the seagull didn't. [5]

Section 3:

Top Gear Live – people come here to watch good stuff too… [6(top), 1(bottom)]

Well it's a living…I could have been an accountant. [1(top), 6(bottom left & bottom right)]

The infamous 'tablecoth shot'. Notice the pattern of the shirt, which looks odd without ketchup stains and a salt cellar on it. Notice also the chubby-cheeked, goofy expression. I fought long and hard to eradicate this shot from the BBC's archives in order to protect my mother and my fragile, bloated, TV presenter's ego. And I did it. I found it and hid it to ensure that it should never again be reproduced in print. Although I have now, of course, just reprinted it again. Bugger. [7]

HMS *Illustrious*. Jimmy Savile never fixed this one. [1]

Illustrious gets her teeth back. [1]

Technical, dynamic and deadly. Shortly afterwards I got drunk, picked a fight with a marine and tried to get into bed with the captain. [1(top & bottom)]

A remarkable band of professionals in a remarkable environment. The officers of HMS *Illustrious* – and me, spot the Wally. [2]

1. Richard Hammond
2. National Geographic Channels International
3. Ben Joiner
4. Gaye Gerard/Getty Images
5. Simon Runting/Rex Features
6. Top Gear Live Ltd
7. © BBC Photo Library

Afraid of Being Forty

There is a very simple solution available to those people who are on telly and who complain about people stopping them in the street because they recognise them: don't be on the telly. Personally, I fail to see how you can be on TV and then complain when people watch it. And so it's part of life's daily goings-on that people will say 'Hi', stop me in the street, ask about people they see me working with on the box, observe that I'm taller/shorter, older/younger in real life than they expected, or beg me to talk to their wife on the phone because 'She really fancies you, mate, and it would make her day if you woke her up and said it was you'. Never quite sure what to do about that last one; a mate of mine suggested I breathe heavily into the receiver and ask what they're wearing. Funny, but slightly inappropriate, and possibly quite dangerous, as it is generally the husband of the woman in question who has asked me to call her and he is standing right next to me. Nevertheless, it happens as a sort of by-product of doing the job and I certainly don't complain about it. And it happens quite a lot in the car.

I tend to scoot about the place in a range of unusual cars; it's part of the job really and it's also one of my biggest passions. I collect all manner of daft motors and so, if I'm not testing some outrageous machine or other for the job, I'll be punting one of my own vehicles about the place, glad of the chance to use it. And, naturally, driving an unusual or distinctive car is going to attract even more attention. The kind of person whose eye is drawn by a Ferrari or a vintage Mustang is going to look at such a car when it appears alongside them on the motorway; and that person is, by definition, likely to be a fan of *Top Gear*. Therefore, if I'm sloping along the M4 in my Morgan Aeromax, people who like cars are going to look at it. And as people who like cars, they are likely to be *Top Gear* viewers and therefore recognise me, perched behind the wheel with one finger jammed firmly up my nose. This happens a lot and on this particular occasion it happened, once again, on the M4 as I made my way out of London towards home in Herefordshire.

A VW Golf – third generation, quite good nick, obviously cared for and therefore probably owned and cherished by a younger driver with a passion for cars – was flitting busily about the big Morgan like a pilot fish around a shark. I caught it changing lanes behind me and then watched it buzz past slowly while its occupants took in the Morgan's outlandish curves. They dropped a window to soak in the noise of the V8 burbling and barking through the side-exit exhausts. I saw young faces, four of them, grinning, in the Golf. They looked along the car to see who was driving such a thing and, sure enough, caught sight of the short one off *Top Gear* and launched into a barrage of shouts and waves. All fair enough. And then they got a bit daft, slowing in the outside lane to drop back along the Morgan and tuck in behind it again. They hovered there for a bit and then found a gap to run up the inside of the car in lane one and undertake me to check out the other side of the Morgan.

I figured this was getting a bit silly and certainly didn't want to be involved in causing anything dangerous to unfold on the motorway. So I gave it a bootful in the Morgan, pulled out into lane three, overtook a few cars and tucked back in, all quiet and cosy. And the Golf caught up to carry on the game, rotating around the car, its occupants all the time grinning and brandishing their upturned thumbs. Clearly, this couldn't continue, so I drifted across into lane one and slowed with the traffic to drop back from the Golf. Gradually, I dropped back further until the blue Golf had disappeared ahead. Better still, an exit road to a service station was coming up. I flicked the indicator on and dived off, slowing into the petrol station. I could do with a tankful and this would give the Golf a chance to get further ahead and out of trouble.

Pulling in alongside a pump, I drew to a halt and climbed out of the car. It's an awkward old thing into and out of which to manoeuvre, the Morgan, and I wrestled myself out on to the forecourt, red-faced and bothered.

Parked in front of me was the same blue Golf I had met earlier. And gathering around it were the four kids who had, only minutes before, been grinning, gawping and giving me an enthusiastic thumbs-up. Only now they didn't look quite so chipper. The largest of them – and therefore, by my reckoning at the time, the eldest and the leader – stepped out of the group towards me. He was all blond, floppy surf hair, white teeth and baggy clothes.

'Hey, Rich!'

His mates giggled at the greeting.

'Sorry about the racing back there.' He jerked a thumb over his shoulder towards the motorway and nodded his head towards the Golf – I assumed the car was his. Something happened inside me, some primal switch or other flicked and I became angry. Not angry in a bar-room brawl kind of way, but angry in an indignant, 'stop this nonsense at once,' kind of way.

'Now listen' – I may just as well have added 'young man', so laden with adult admonishment of a junior was my tone of delivery – 'that was not racing. For one thing, it's a public motorway and why the hell do you think I would race against you when there's a very real chance someone entirely innocent could be killed? If anyone even thought we were actually racing I would be arrested quicker than you can think about it and fired from my job immediately, and rightly bloody so.'

The young man in question lowered his eyes and looked suddenly sheepish. As did his entire group. They were, I realised, a rather foppish, middle-class, pleasant bunch of lads, probably from a posh school. They wore rugby shirts and deck shoes. They felt bad at being shouted at.

'And anyway,' I blustered now, feeling suddenly awkward, though not quite sure why, 'if we actually were racing and I was in that', I nodded at the big Morgan, cooling quietly by the petrol pump, 'do you really think you'd stand any kind of chance? Hah, I mean …'

I tried to inject some matey levity and banter into the situation, but it didn't work. The lads were cowed, browbeaten. And I realised where my sudden awkwardness had sprung from: they were taking my admonishment as exactly that: a bollocking. And yet here was a bunch of strapping young lads, any one of whom could have picked me up and bundled me out of the way as easily as dealing out a tackle on a rugby pitch. I scanned their faces instinctively, acting on a lifetime of waiting to see which punter in my local would be the first to throw a punch at my irritating little face. But nothing flickered, not a trace of anger or danger. They looked down at their feet and muttered their apologies. They were, I realised, apologising naturally to the older man, feeling shameful and sorry. They viewed me as an adult crashing into their young man's world and telling them to stop being so silly. I wasn't ready for this. It's my age, it's because I'm forty soon – have I mentioned that? – and I don't yet want to be the indignant older bloke at the petrol station who shouts at teenagers and expects to get their respect simply by dint of being older.

'Anyway lads, er, take it easy out there.' I punched the air at about waist height as I spoke, giving the non-contact equivalent of a chuck on the shoulder. I may as well have put on a bad tie and danced like a twat at a wedding disco.

'Sorry,' one of them muttered in gentle, polished tones and they returned to their car, shuffling quietly, heads slightly bowed, their buoyant mood burst by my middle-age sensitivities. And so the nearly-forty-year-old-man climbed back into his sports car, surveyed the sparkling dashboard, sporty dials and bucket seats and denied to himself that he was having a mid-life crisis. Then he fired up the big V8 and gunned it to send pops and bangs ricocheting off the walls of the filling station and powered back towards the motorway. If I'm going to have a mid-life crisis, may as well do it properly. And loudly.

Or is that just me?

Chapter One

There's No Snow in Hawaii, Surely?

'It's about fourteen thousand feet, which is about the same as when you go skiing. Do you go skiing?'

'No, look, for the last time, I don't go and never have been skiing. Well, I did once, but that was to the North Pole and that was different because it wasn't downhill and the dogs kept peeing on me and, oh God …' I tentatively patted the point where a large and visibly very angry spot had recently set up camp, presumably mistaking me for a teenager. In the few days since its arrival I had grown accustomed to reaching up and checking it, testing the tautness of the skin stretched across its shining, ominous dome. I was fearful that it might appear unsightly on camera. Mindy had laughed and told me that it might get fan mail. And that people would wonder if I had the spot or the spot had me. Was it, she asked, in fact wearing me, stuck to its little bottom? Was I a boil on the bum of a spot? She told me to stop touching it because this, she added, would make it bigger. I protested that spots don't thrive on being petted. They are not Labradors. She spoke testily about the transfer of germs and grease and other unmentionable things. Eventually the three of us — the spot, Mindy and me — had agreed on a standoff. We would all try to get along together as best we could: I wouldn't pick at the spot, Mindy wouldn't keep asking me if it made a noise at night and the spot itself, though we had to make this assumption on its behalf as communication was not among the wealth of qualities it brought to our unhappy triumvirate, would not erupt like Vesuvius on camera, leaving a TV studio ruined and a generation of children traumatised for life by the horror.

'Don't touch it ...' Mindy hissed the words at me in a stage whisper, standing to my left with a mug of tea in one hand and a single riding boot in the other, listening in to my conversation as I dealt with the intricacies of planning another filming trip abroad.

'All right, all right.' I mouthed the words and waved her away loftily, striving to give the impression that my mind was busy dealing with important professional matters.

'What? Never! You don't ski? God, I go every year and it's soooo ...'

The young researcher on the other end of the phone was in danger of slipping into the stereotypical waffle about how she goes skiing every year with her friends and it's just great and little Toby, my godson, looks so cute in his little ski suit and when I have kids I'll, y'know, make sure they can ski by the time they're three and .... I decided on a pre-emptive strike and interrupted her before things turned too grisly.

'Look, I was born in Birmingham; people from Birmingham didn't go skiing, they went camping in the Forest of Dean. James Bond went skiing. And people in car ads. Real people in the real world went camping. We took the tent, the deck chairs and the camping stove out of the shed where they had gone mouldy and rusty, we strapped them all to the top of the Marina, we drove for hours and hours and hours, we argued about where to pitch the tent when we got there, we got wet putting it up in the rain, argued about who's turn it was to wash up, argued about who had lost a playing card and ruined the pack, slept on a damp groundsheet and went home. So, please, stop asking me about skiing.'

'Okay, well, er …' She wasn't sure if my rant was meant in jest or if I was genuinely cross.

'And we had to eat gravel and grass and, ooooh, we had it bad back then.' I added the coda with pantomime emphasis to make it clear that I was having fun with her. I wasn't; it had made me a bit cross, but I didn't see the need for her to know that.

Reassured, she continued, 'At that altitude you to have to be a bit careful because the air's thin and you can get altitude sickness …' The young researcher swung into a lecture about the need to stay off the booze and fags while we were up there and how we would need to make sure we took the time to acclimatise on every trip to the top of the mountain. She lectured me about the impor-tance of watching for symptoms, about how a headache can be the first sign of the onset of altitude sickness. I zoned out and made the appropriate noises during the quiet bits to indicate that I was listening intently and taking on board the critical, possibly life-saving information I was being given. It's not that I wasn't interested or was being blasé about serious stuff, but I knew that we would go through all of this again and again over the next few weeks and it would be well covered before we set off. Right now I was more concerned about what we were actually going up this mountain, wherever it was, to film.

This was to be just one of a series of journeys I was involved in making for a new series for the National Geographic Channel. Called *Engineering Connections*, it would look at the unlikely and unexpected stories connecting major technological structures and achievements of the modern age with older, stranger, simpler and altogether wilder stuff from around the world. When first invited to host it, the producers asked me if I remembered the original series, presented by James Burke in the 1970s. Of course I did, I reassured them. A man with my scientific credentials was hardly likely to have failed to observe a truly landmark television series in the field of science communication.

'God, yes, of course; part of my childhood. A founding stone of it, in fact. Michael Burke, sorry, James, huh, how could I forget? He was my hero. No, James, James Burke walked up and down a lot of streets wearing a suit and talked about how jet fighters are actually directly descended from letterboxes. And stuff. I loved it. When do we start?'

And it had indeed made for some fascinating work. In the course of filming an episode about the Airbus A380

airliner, I had found myself charging out of some woodland on a horse, with a bow in my hand, firing arrows
into an archery target in front of a slightly bewildered
archery club from Middlesex. It was part of a stunt to
explore the properties of the groundbreaking high-tech
material from which the plane is built. Called Glare, it is
made rather like fibreglass, from two different substances
that have different qualities which when combined make
a material capable of more than the constituent parts on
their own. The Mongol army of Genghis Khan did something rather similar with its bows. As a mounted army, it
needed weapons that could be used from horseback. A
traditional longbow was a bit too, well, long to use on a
horse. You tended to stick the end of it in the horse's
back, which sort of made it cross, and caused it to chuck
you off and look a right prat in front of the enemy, who
killed you where you lay with knives or clubs. And on
this particular day's filming, somewhere in Middlesex, I
had already demonstrated this problem – not the being
killed with knives and/or clubs bit, but I had shown the
difficulties of manhandling a five-foot-long bow on
horseback by being filmed trying to loose off an arrow
using a full-sized wooden longbow. It was impossible, and
the crew were relieved when I put the bow down and
admitted defeat. They had feared one of them would lose
an eye. The Mongols, clever chaps, noticed that if you just
made a wooden bow shorter, it snapped in half when you
tried to pull it back far enough to get sufficient tension
into it to send an arrow further than the end of your
wrist. That was because on one side of the bow, the for-

11

ward-facing bit, you're asking the wood to stretch as it forms the outside of the curve. That puts the material under tension. On the other side, the inside, it's being squashed, compressed, as the bow bends inwards. And that's quite a big ask of one material; to manage to be good at two completely opposing jobs – tension and compression. So the Mongols made a bow using two very different materials. On the outside they used sinew taken from an animal carcass, typically the leg tendon of a deer, which is naturally very good at stretching and returning to its original shape without breaking. On the inside, they used water buffalo horn, which is very good at being squashed. And it worked a treat. The bow needed only to be about three feet long and yet could send an arrow hundreds of yards with marvellous accuracy. The Mongols, as well as being fearsome warriors with a bloody reputation, were a pretty brainy lot, as it turned out, sort of warrior boffins, with their neat, high-tech little bow. They murdered millions with it. Obviously, that last bit strikes a bit of a sombre note, but it was very, very clever and really the origin of modern composites like carbon fibre. Unlike our more recent response to the invention of carbon fibre, the Mongols didn't then go on to buy sheets of plastic made to look a bit like their new composite material and then stick them all over their hot hatches because they believed their friends would then think their 1.2 litre Nova was a Formula 1 car.

So I wobbled about on horseback, waving a replica Mongol warrior bow around and explaining all of this stuff, while the crew hid in the trees and crapped themselves laughing at my ropey horsemanship. We needed to demonstrate just how significant a development this was in a historical context and, to set the scene, had invited a local archery club down to the airfield where we were filming. They would take part in a scene in which they would play humble, foot-bound archers. and I would crash majestically from the woods as a fearless Mongol warrior, master of horse, bow and terror. It was going to be a bit tricky playing my part authentically, though, as Health and Safety had insisted on me wearing a riding hat. This was never part of a Mongol warrior's battle dress and did rather stand out. Particularly when the archery club members had really gone for it and turned up in clothing that more closely resembled their ancestors' - a sea of imitation leather jerkins and archer's wrist guards. I wore jeans, a green jacket from Cheltenham and a blue riding hat with a plastic bit down the middle. On a given signal, I was to ride the horse out of the woods as the archers milled about in front of the target attempting to impersonate an angry mob armed with longbows. They made slightly embarrassed, middle-class noises while I tried to persuade the black Friesian stunt horse I had been loaned to transport me out of the trees in a heroic fashion. The riding hat was a couple of sizes too big and wobbled about on my head as the horse, out of spite, took me under the lowest branches at the fringes of the wood. The archers were now doing what they had been briefed to do earlier in the day by a tired and harassed director, loading up their bows (or notching their arrows, as is, I believe, the correct term) and letting loose a fearsome flurry at the straw target perched on a wooden stand at the edge of the clearing. Obviously, Mongol warriors didn't spend much of their time interrupting provincial archery club competitions in southern England, but to ship me, the crew and a horse out to the Mongolian steppe just to film a two-minute segment of a programme about an aeroplane would have stretched the budget rather. So I steeled my nerves and tried to look fierce and heroic. The horse wandered out of the woods and stood at the edge of the clearing chewing at a leaf it had grabbed from an overhead branch. I wrestled with the chinstrap of my oversized riding hat and shifted in the saddle awkwardly. The script now called for me to crash out of the woods on the black charger, prance fearsomely in front of the archers on the ground and loose a lethal volley of arrows into the target before spinning and galloping away, presumably to enjoy whatever massive drink-fuelled, sex-charged party your average Mongol warrior tucked into after a bit of raiding and conquering. This would conclusively demonstrate the deadly superiority that the Mongol war bow, with its forward-thinking composite construction, gave the horse-mounted archer over the traditional archer on foot. Obviously it was quite important that the archery club stop their firing at this point, lest the horse and I wander into their lethal hailstorm and be reduced to pincushions. The owner of the horse would be quite angry about this. The horse was, it had been pointed out to me in no uncertain terms, a very expensive horse. He had previously been ridden by Johnny Depp. Or Orlando Bloom. Or Michael Caine.

Someone very famous had ridden him in a film, anyway. And I was made to feel that it was indeed an honour for my low-rent, humble television butt to be allowed to rest on the back of a creature that had supported the stellar cheeks of some Hollywood luminary.

Right now, though, as I watched the archery club's 'lethal' volley flop from their bows and land on the ground a yard or two in front of them, I wondered if it might just save time if I rode out in front of them anyway and took my chances. Their arrows, launched with the ferocity and pinpoint accuracy of a bin-bound chip wrapper, looked as if they would have had trouble piercing a hole in a crepe paper modesty screen. As the horse and I pawed and snorted at the edge of the wood awaiting our cue, I noticed a middle-aged woman halfway along the line notch an arrow carefully, her tongue sticking out with the effort of steadying her hands as she put the string into the notch behind the feathered flights. She raised the bow and drew back the arrow. Her arms shook, the string moved back three or four inches, most of the shaft of the arrow still pro-truding from the front of the bow at an unpromising angle. She closed her eyes, turned her head to one side as though expecting a shotgun's retort and released the bowstring. The arrow flopped sideways out of the bow and fell on her feet.

This was not quite the hailstorm of steel-tipped death I had envisaged. I had told Mindy what I was doing that day and she had begged me to be careful. Highly strung black stallions can be very difficult, she had warned me, and doing stunt work on horseback is dangerous – I may have dressed it up a bit as we sat with a bottle of wine the night before I left. This scene, as it was playing out now, was not going to impress her. I kicked the horse on, and moved out across the clearing. The target lay off to my left; the archers were gathered by some low bushes to my right. They saw me moving out of the woods and low-ered their bows and ceased fire. A couple of arrows lay on the ground at the foot of the target. One had actually penetrated the straw of the target itself and stuck out of it now, a lone salute to one archer's competency. The horse would, I had been told by the patient but not, I could tell, impressed handler, respond very well to input from my legs. I dropped the reins and lifting the bow in my left hand, notched an arrow into the thick string with my right. I used my legs to put the horse into a gentle right turn and as we trotted away from the target I twisted in the saddle, bringing the tip of the arrow into line with the target, tensioned the string and then released it. The arrow leapt from the bow and, with a sin-ister and satisfying whistle, hurtled towards the target, burying its metal beak in the round straw face. The archers, in front of me now as I legged the horse through the rest of our long, curving turn, were silenced. No comments or even abuse floated up from the crew either, their tripod and sound boom standing black and angular at the edge of the field. The plan called for me to loose a whole quiverful of arrows at the target. The camera would pick up shots as I repeated each manoeuvre and the best bits would, in the time-honoured fashion, be

strung together in the final sequence. I turned the horse
further to the right, bringing us out of the curve and now
parallel with the target. There are four positions used to
fire from horseback: you can fire off to the right of the
horse's head, off to the left, a broadside directly perpendicular to the length of the horse and then, finally, turn in
the saddle and fire backwards as you ride away. This was
the 'parting shot'. I ran through the lot of them, blazing
away with the bow from each of the accepted positions.
It was an absolute bloody doddle and unbelievably good
fun. There is, sadly, no national governing body for the
sport of mounted archery – it isn't a national sport.
Which is a monumental shame. Apart from the near certainty that someone, either participant or spectator, will
end up with an arrow sticking out of his or her face, it is
something all of us should be doing every weekend. I can
think of nothing finer to do of a crisp Sunday morning
than riding out to your local park, pinning a target to a
tree, sneaking up on it on horseback and blazing away
with a Mongol war bow. You could team up with a mate
and devise a point-scoring system for accuracy, grouping
and speed of delivery. Picnickers and the like might moan
a bit, but what exactly is the point of such public spaces
if they are not for members of the public to use for the
pursuit of their chosen activities, whatever they may be,
without being harassed and persecuted just for blinding
or maiming a few idle pork pie noshers and surprising
the odd squirrel?

And now, just a few weeks after inventing a new
national sport – that, admittedly, has yet to catch on in a

big way, but give it time – I was planning a trip to film another *Engineering Connections* programme. This one would feature the Keck Observatory, home to the most powerful telescope in the world, and capable of taking us further into the depths of space than ever before. We would film the links and associated stories later, and they would include setting fire to boats with an ancient Greek mirror and carving my name across the width of a single hair using an atom-blasting microscope, but, first, we had to visit the telescope itself and film the piece of astonishing technology at the centre of the story. All very exciting stuff that was made, it must be said, only more exciting by the fact that the telescope was based, not on some dismal mountain range in Wales or the Arctic Circle, but on the island of Hawaii. In the course of a bit of background reading I discovered that the 'scope had not been sited there to facilitate a spot of fun in the sun for the astronomers. The island had been chosen because on it is an extinct volcano, Mauna Kea, which stands nearly 14,000 feet high and this altitude is one of the many factors that come together to make Mauna Kea such a prized site for boffins with big telescopes. I quickly found that the benefit of setting up your telescope at high altitude doesn't come about because you're a bit closer to your subject, the stars. You *are* closer, of course, but proportionally it makes as much difference as standing on a chair to wave at the moon. I was glad to have cleared that one up before I set off to interview the brain boxes operating the telescope. I absolutely would have asked how much it helped being a bit closer to the stars. And they

18

would have thought me an idiot. And been right. The altitude helps because the air is thinner up there, giving the telescope a better chance of peering out through the atmosphere and into space. This factor, together with the absence of light pollution – given the island's solitary position, far from big cities – and the stable winds coming in off the Pacific make it one of the world's absolute best locations for setting up observatories. It bristles with them in fact, with universities and companies from all over the world competing to set up telescopes using all manner of modern technologies to see further and further out into the universe. My hopes of a couple of weeks in the sun, looking at hula girls and drinking coconut milk were somewhat dashed when I saw photographs of the ice-clad summit of Mauna Kea where the observatories huddle together; so many hunched domes sheltering in the thin, freezing air. This was to be my home for a fortnight. Could be worse. Could have turned out that the perfect conditions all came together to make Burnley the best place to build a telescope. And as for the freezing weather up there, well, I'm not a fan of Bermuda shorts anyway and I still had all the kit I'd bought for our *Top Gear* trip to the Pole, so I could, at least, turn up looking the part.

*

There was a slight twinge, experienced by all of us in the team, as we landed in Hawaii and caught glimpses of the legendary beaches, sparkling blue seas and swaying palms of this classic jewel in the ocean. We were not many in our team for our assault on Mauna Kea, but we had worked together before and were happy that, between us, we could more than do the job. But any ideas that we were about to spend a few days together posing with TV cameras on a palm-fringed beach were slowly withering.

The hotel was not going to be glamorous; I was prepared for that. I was glad of it, even. This was very much a proper, working trip. We were there to make a grownup documentary about the most powerful telescope in the world. It was to be screened by the National Geographic Channel in America and across the world. Every fact in it would be thoroughly researched and checked against three different sources to be sure of its validity. This was certainly not a *Top Gear* shoot. At no point was I going to be challenged by the producers to drive across a lake in a dustbin lorry or join the Le Mans 24 Hour race in a canoe. And so it felt immediately appropriate when our hired minibus dropped us and our mountain of kit off in the car park of a low-lying concrete and wood building that looked like something members of a school field trip might stay in. I stepped from the bus and tried to show willing as Pete, the cameraman, marshalled the filming kit coming out of the back of the lorry into the all too familiar mound of shining aluminium cases, sinister black boxes and battered bags. Grant hefted me a tripod out of the back of the bus like he was hefting coal into a steam train's boiler. He looked up and smiled as I grabbed the heavy end of the bulky metal tripod.

'Nice place Hawaii.' I nodded at the bleak hills surrounding the hollow where our utilitarian, single-storey hostel sheltered.

'Bit like North Wales.'

Grant laughed, his face muscles pulled taught across a grin that showed he was enjoying the ridiculous reality of arriving on an island synonymous with beaches, sun and sand dressed in duck-down parka and Arctic mitts.

It was cold. I wore a thick jacket over thermals and woollens and still felt its bite. And we were barely halfway up the mountain yet. It would get a lot colder before we reached the top and finally came face to face with the machine we had travelled to see. I breathed deeply, closing my eyes with concentration as I tried to detect any difference in the oxygen content of the air. We were high but the observatory was much higher still, at 13,600 feet. But the effects of altitude can, I had been told in several lectures from the production team, be felt from as low as 7,000 feet. Any combination of headaches, nausea, loss of appetite, insomnia, extreme shortness of breath, coughing, congestion, disorientation and difficulty with thought processes were all possible, but a headache was the first sign. The worst affected could develop high-altitude pulmonary oedema as fluid collects in the lungs which, if not treated swiftly, could lead to death. I knew that on Michael Palin's epic journey through the Himalayas the sound man had contracted pulmonary oedema and had to be airlifted to hospital. With these thoughts swirling round my head I unpacked and went to bed.

Once you've been told that a headache is possible, there's room inside your head for little else. Your mind becomes hypersensitised to the idea that it is soon to be under attack from some external force as fierce as a tiger and as big as Tyrannosaurus Rex. A thought is a light, floaty sort of thing; it doesn't weigh much. But every one landed in my head that morning as though it were a sackful of builder's rubble. I swivelled my eyes about the room, taking in the dull walls, utilitarian melamine furniture and beige curtains covering a window beyond which I knew stretched a landscape eerily like North Wales and I tried to mentally probe the space in my head for headaches. I imagined myself opening every cupboard in there, every desk drawer. I ranged the corridors and floors, kicking open doors and shouting 'freeze, it's a raid' as gangs of thoughts looked up in fear at this angry intruder. A bunch of lecherous fantasies, grey and greasy in their guilt, looked up languorously as I burst through one door. They held playing cards close to their chests and looked like fish with their round, flat eyes and bulbous, dead lips. I found many things in that room, some of them quite bad, but no headaches. I wandered through memories, motor responses, reactions and emotions and found nothing. The space was clear for now. So it was just a case of waiting, before the headache arrived.

The daylight from the small, square window behind thin, beige curtains shone through bright and colourless. The room had that practical, institutional feel that is welcoming in its lack of pretension but somehow threatening by association. It recalled the kind of prison cell I've seen on telly where you end up shouting that they're having a better life than you, the innocent TV viewer, with their clean beds, pleasant bedside cabinets and smart wardrobes. And it's not surprising that we sometimes feel like that. Especially when we are struggling our arses off to support ourselves as a freelance radio reporter, earning just enough to live in a miserable one-room bedsit in Carlisle, with only a battered sofa, a 1970s black and white television and a camping stove for company and then, on that same, ancient TV, we are forced to watch some miserable thieving little sod sit and chat with his mates in a prison cell – paid for from the taxes screwed out of our pitiful paycheck before we've even seen it – with a proper colour telly, a nice view of the grounds and a Pirelli calendar on the neatly painted bloody walls. Or is that just me? They swirled on, unbidden: I mean, I'm not suggesting hard labour or anything, but bloody hell; it's a bit hard to swallow when, as a twenty-year-old, full of big plans for your life but broke and lonely, you see people who couldn't be bothered to try and learn how to do anything to earn a living but nicked someone's car instead, moaning on about how it was 'because of the drugs' and the need to 'feed' their habit that they nicked the car and that it's actually society's fault for letting them down. Well, yes, and perhaps to salve its conscience that same society pays for the little scamp to live in comfort and convenience while getting over the letdown. So who's paying the price for the crime? I didn't have much to think about in my bedsit and tended to get quite cross.

A low chest of drawers stood to one side of the window and my rucksack slouched on top of it, disgorging more of its contents than I had intended to unpack the night before when I had grabbed my washbag and towel. The room reminded me of somewhere specific and I struggled to drag up the memory, fearful all the time of opening a door in all innocence only to be pounced upon by the dreaded altitude headache, sure to be followed by almost certain death.

I found it. The memory had been there all along, loitering in the foreground while I rummaged about at the back. And it wasn't the decor or the furniture; it was the view beyond the window, it reminded me of Wales. I had opened the curtains the previous evening to look out across a landscape pocked with black rocks and sharp, angular little plains. The hill we were on swept down towards a broad valley that ran across my view, perpendicular to the window. A road ribboned along its bottom, a thin black snake against a pale, grassy backdrop. Somewhere ahead lay the snowline and the ground slowly feathered from pale and grassy to the high-contrast, white rolling hills of the mountain itself. Volcanic rocks and snow combined to make a black-and-white scene, one thrown into stark relief against the other. This was a place I would like, I decided. I am comfortable among damp, heavy hills, far more comfortable, in fact, than I ever am wandering aimlessly along some stretch of beach littered with people wearing flip-flops. I'm a hill person, always have been.

My school had an old cottage in Snowdonia where

pupils were sent to spend a week when they reached the second year. Ostensibly it was to learn about geology. We visited hydroelectric projects and spoke about glacial valleys and moraines. We packed lunches and ate them on bleak hillsides, savouring thin ham and mustard between damp slices of white bread. I was in my element; I loved the hills, loved walking and loved the bad weather. I could talk authoritatively about pathfinding and map reading, enjoying my superiority when other boys struggled with their Sylva compasses and grid references. And it was then that I took part in the only sustained and deliberate act of bullying I have ever been involved with. I still shudder at the memory. One lad, as is always the case in a bunch made up exclusively of young males – and females too probably, though I have never been able to be in an exclusively female group, obviously, so can't talk from experience – was the 'victim'. He was picked on constantly, made fun of, blamed when things went wrong and generally abused. It was the usual playground fun, but I think of it still when I am being picked on and hope he found it in his heart to forgive us for what we did on our trip to Snowdonia in the second year of our school lives together. It was bloody funny, though. This wasn't a piece of physical bullying; nobody stole anyone else's dinner money or beat them up. Though that did happen, unsurprisingly, to this same lad.

The torture began one evening as we lay in our dorm in the Welsh cottage. There were three sets of bunk beds in our room, so six sleepers in all. Morton, the lad in the bunk above mine, had just stabbed me and we were still laughing as I sucked the blood from my thumb. I say 'stabbed'; that is how we viewed it at the time, though an accident is probably a better description of the event. I was and am an inveterate knife collector. I don't carry one on me. I have never intended using a knife to extort money from strangers or to hold up a bank. I just like knives. I enjoy their simplicity as a tool, acknowledge their significance to the human species and can savour their elegance of construction. And they appealed to me then, so I had taken with me a handsome folding pocketknife with brass ends and a wooden handle. It locked open with a satisfying click and stayed open until you thumbed a metal ridge standing proud of a curved cut-out on the back and unlocked the blade to fold it shut. The metal was thick and shiny. I had used Brasso to buff up the ends. The wooden grips were punctuated by three rivets, holding them in place along the sides of the knife. The whole thing was weighty and substantial. And Morton nicked it. Well, he borrowed it. We had been fighting, throwing pillows, practising swearing and basically just being boys. The fight had eventually subsided and I found that by pressing against the bottom of Morton's bunk, which was above mine, with my feet, I could make his life truly uncomfortable. I tried shoving as hard as I could, bracing my feet against the cold metal springs above my head and pushing with all my might. Morton laughed loudly as his mattress bulged upwards and threatened to throw him off, on to the hard floor below. I saw an arm reach down from above; he must have been holding the rail at the head of the bunk with his other hand to steady himself as he reached down to the simple, wooden chest alongside our bed. Something flashed past in the low light from the lamp on the chest. He had taken my knife. I heard it click open and then, with a yell, Morton started stabbing furiously down the side of the bed, between his bunk and the wall. He made a screeching noise reminiscent of the infamous shower scene in *Psycho*. The others laughed. Morton often pretended to go entirely bonkers; it was one of his trademarks and we liked him for it. The stubby, shining blade of the knife bit away at the air below Morton's bunk and above mine. I shouted that it was my knife and, without thinking, reached up and grabbed the blade as it appeared between Morton's bunk and the wall. Feeling the pull on the knife, Morton instinctively retracted it and, not surprisingly, the blade slid through the soft flesh of my thumb. It wasn't a bad cut, not much more than a paper cut really, but it was a knife wound and therefore the subject of much close scrutiny over the next half an hour as we gathered round the table in the centre of our dorm and, in low, earnest voices discussed knife fights and stabbings we had witnessed – a limited number really, given that we were all from the pleasant, leafy suburbs of Solihull. The blood flow stemmed and our talk exhausted, we dispersed back to our beds, each clambering up to the top or falling gratefully to the bottom bunk with what we hoped were manly sighs of weariness. And then, at some point in the quiet gloom, Morton had his great idea. He introduced it gradually with a moan or two.

'You all right, mate?' I asked into the night.

'Yeah. Cramp though, bad one.'

'Er, right.'

'I get 'em. Y'know, every month. Terrible.' He moaned again.

'Yeah.' I sensed a game was afoot, though didn't yet know what.

'You get them? Cramps? Or you get headaches. Y'know, time of the month and everything.' And in a flash I had it. We were, inevitably, fascinated with all things biological. Although obviously only what we saw as the rude bits actually held our attention; we weren't that fussed about asexual reproduction though it seemed to most of us a pretty efficient way of going about things. And one of our group, through an older sister probably, had brought to us earlier that week the news that women had some sort of bicycle thing that they suffered with every month and that gave them headaches and made them feel ill. It was all connected somehow to having babies and got a bit complicated, so we gave up on it. But Morton clearly had other ideas.

'Oh, I get a bit of both really. Sort of a headache and the cramps. Nasty, though. Bad luck that yours came now.'

'Yeah, well, I knew it would. But what could I do?' Morton groaned again and shifted on his bunk, flexing the metal springs above my head. From the other side of the room, another boy, also picking up on the game, joined in.

'I get headaches, too. Terrible. Really bad ones, have to lie in a dark room and everything.'

More were getting it now and joining in, reedy voices,

half broken and raspy, a chorus of tales of headaches, stomach cramps and misery. I recognised every voice, heard from all present, apart from one. The natural victim of our group had not joined in. I spoke loudly to ask him across the room if he too suffered with cramps or headaches. He made a non-committal noise and I heard his bed squeak as he turned over. Awake then, but not biting at the bait yet. Morton moaned again. The rest of the room lay silent and I sensed that he was going for the *coup de grâce*. He was not a natural bully, Morton, just a clever lad who could use his mind and humour to entertain his friends. If the entertainment of the majority came at the expense of one, then so be it.

'There are some kids, y'know, who don't get 'em. Who never start.' I held my breath, stifling a laugh, and felt others do the same around me.

'And here's the thing. They keep it from them. Never tell 'em that there's something wrong.'

This was getting better by the second. Surely, though, this wouldn't work. He'd never fall for this; some sort of national conspiracy involving parents and teachers successfully hiding from kids what would be, if it were true, a pretty major piece of our natural lives.

'And if they don't, y'know, *start*,' Morton emphasised the word, loading it with meaning and significance to convey the importance of the 'start' he was talking about, 'it means they're gay.'

I bit down on my lip now, anxious not to give the game away and ruin whatever fragile chance it had of fooling our victim.

'Oh, yes, I've heard that, actually.' Another boy joined in now, trying perhaps too hard to keep his voice relaxed and chatty, but nevertheless giving it his best shot to add to the lie being carefully woven by Morton, above my head in his bunk.

'If they haven't started', again the heavy emphasis on the word 'started', 'by the time they're twelve, then that's it, definitely gay. That's how they know.'

Needless to say, calling someone 'gay' in a West Midlands boys' school was a pretty high charge. I was not aware of ever having met anyone who genuinely could answer the charge in the affirmative. And this, perhaps, is an indication of just how grim life must have been then for anyone slowly coming to the realisation that they were not like most people in their class. They would have been present, naturally, but keeping their heads down and their secret clutched very close to their chest. Talking to gay friends about it now, it sounds as though, for some, the early eighties was a tortured and troubled time filled with straightforward prejudice spilling over sometimes into active persecution. None of us actually understood anything of what it meant and it was just a term of derision and disdain, devoid really of meaning beyond saying someone was different from the rest of the gang. We might just as readily use terms referring to physical differences, racial differences or qualities. What we meant, I guess, was 'outsider'. And to be put outside the tight-knit pack that is any group of young boys together, anywhere, is something desperately to be avoided. Conform or be cast out is the rule. And in being complicit in this cruel new joke I was certainly conforming.

'I heard that they really don't know, y'know? That they really do get to be like thirteen or even older before they realise that they haven't started and they're gay.'

Yet another voice chimed in, the joke now spreading across the dorm, bringing others in. We carried on for a bit, telling tales of headaches and stomach cramps, of feeling angry and sad and confused and of dreading its monthly arrival. And not once did we hear the thin, piping voice of our victim. But we heard him shuffle in his bedclothes, shifting uneasily, I guessed, under the weight of attention that was being focused on him by those talking around the dimly lit dorm. And later that night, among the snores and snuffles of my roommates, I heard him cry. A muffled, muted sob, smothered by a pillow, came from the corner where I knew our victim's bunk to be. And I was ashamed of my complicity, my weakness and of our collective cruelty. I still am, actually; it was a pretty rotten trick and what hurt, I suspect, was not the story itself – he was a clever lad, as I recall, and unlikely to fall for a tale of male menstruation being kept from an entire tranche of the population and being a subsequent indicator of their sexual orientation – but the fact that every other boy in the room with him could join in and try to fool him with it. It wasn't the story, it was the telling of it that wounded him, I suppose. I gave up bullying that day. Never really had the opportunity to do it again anyway.

*

I didn't get any of the symptoms of altitude sickness, sitting in my bland, beige bedroom halfway up a Hawaiian volcano. Shame really; it would have lent a certain glamour to the occasion. Instead, I slept deeply, woke early and went for a brief run, keen to experience the extra benefits of training in a thin-air environment. I had read that athletes sometimes travel to such places to work on their cardiovascular performance, taking their finely honed bodies to new levels of efficiency. I trotted about a bit, ran up the sloping ride for a mile or two and felt maybe very slightly woozy. That was it.

Our team met for breakfast in what the hotel called the 'canteen', presumably trying to give it a brisk, businesslike feel and at the same time excuse the basic, functional status of the room. A man in late middle age wearing a white apron round his waist and a shirt with big black-and-white checks stood behind the counter dispensing baked potatoes, salads and sponge puddings in the evenings and plates of undercooked bacon and over-cooked eggs in the mornings. This, clearly, was the kind of place where brainy but tough and outdoorsy astronomers based themselves when they came to spend months carrying out essential observations at the very edge of the universe. And they didn't care too much about the food while they did it. The canteen was next to a casual sitting area. This really was a sixth formers' common room with low wooden bookshelves around the outside, mismatched sofas, two large, low tables and a dartboard. We sat and drank instant coffee while planning our first day at the telescope. I was distracted by the thought that, at some point, I just knew that one of the astronomers, a really wacky, zany one, would produce an acoustic guitar in this room and entertain the others with renditions of Beach Boys classics. I shuddered at the thought of it and failed to take in much of the briefing. But it wasn't really for me anyway. I knew what I wanted to say; all we had to do was get me there, prop me up in front of the camera and record me saying it. How difficult could this be anyway? It was only a bloody telescope.

With the kit loaded up in our hired SUVs, we covered the last few miles to the summit. The snow grew deeper and smoothed away the mountain's finer contours. The sky was now an evenly diffused white, the light losing its dawn tinges of pink and orange to be replaced by thin cloud. As we reached the summit, we saw the first observatories: silver domes atop white buildings hunched in the snow, each separated by a few hundred yards, cradled by the hill's soft curves. With their shutters closed, they looked intensely private, looking inward rather than outward to the skies they were sited there to observe. It was a landscape as alien to my eyes as the planets I assumed these silent, shy eyes could study in detail fine enough to watch their counterparts, if they existed, looking balefully back at them. Our telescope, the W. M. Keck Observatory, was the largest, a fact indicated by the presence of not one, but two vast white domes on a site at the very crest of the mountain.

The astronomers we met there were a close team; a more tightly-knit bunch, even, than me and my mates working as a pack back at the school cottage in Wales nearly three decades ago. As we moved amongst them and caught snippets of conversation and chat, you could identify the timid ones, the funny ones and, inevitably, the bullies or, as they must be labelled in the adult world, the 'Alpha Males'. Which is nothing more than a flash title for school bullies who shave and can vote and use their adult cunning to play mind games that are every bit as effective at suppressing and intimidating the people around them without actually having to go to all the trouble of giving them a dead-leg and stealing their dinner money every day. In their eerie, isolated world, I could see how the usual human traits and characteristics could be emphasized and exaggerated in the long, lonely nights of observation.

The buildings which serve the observatory are punctuated by long, cluttered corridors, opening up into the vast chambers of the telescope rooms themselves. It was easy to let your imagination go in this tightly-knit world, to quickly give extreme tendencies to the team which served the telescopes. I imagined gangs of astronomers hanging out at strategic corners like gum-chewing, leather-jacketed characters in a musical. There was, inevitably a leader; there always is. One of the astronomers possessed an air of arrogance and a physical presence sufficient to dominate the others. Quick-witted and bright, he could keep up with any technical conversation going on around him, but it was clear too that a large part of whatever intellect he possessed was dedicated to the demonstration of the prowess and superiority of that same intellect to those around him. If jokes were being shared, he took no pleasure from the sharing but would come up with the most extreme. If the discussion turned to matters historical, technical or philosophical, he would blunder about the conversation in ugly, staccato bursts looking for opportunities, not to contribute to the exploration of ideas and concepts, but for chances to slip in a few of the many facts, names and dates his avaricious mind had caught and held onto solely for the purpose, once again, of demonstrating its power and scale to those he met. He was, in short, the observatory's Alpha-Male-in-residence. He had acolytes; characters he kept close around him and variously they would entertain, flatter or compliment him and contribute to the overall effect of this place being something of a unique wilderness, a hothouse amongst the snow-capped peaks of Mauna Kea.

As we filmed our general shots, harvested our brief interviews with the observers and recorded my pieces to camera to complete our film, we discussed what the place would be like when we weren't there recording everything. There was no one from the outside world to patrol these corridors, no one to keep order amongst the denizens of this world apart and keep, perhaps, their feet on the ground as their eyes and minds strained upwards into the far reaches of the universe. We imagined complex initiation ceremonies being held for terrified new arrivals joining the team. We wondered what cruel punishments the Alpha Male, the Lord of the Flies, would deal out to keep order and keep himself at the head of the pack; what political friendships he would negotiate amongst the others and how quickly they might end when they no longer served his purpose. We finished our recording and we left them. They are still there, staring into space. But it is what goes on at the other end of their telescopes that still tugs at my imagination. I would love to visit there again, at night, when the telescopes are working. But I don't think I would visit alone.

Chapter Two

Falling Apart

The doctor invited me into the bathroom and there he performed acts upon my person intimate enough to be considered close to illegal in many countries. He had arrived at our tiny London flat barely ten minutes earlier, summoned by an anxious phone call from Mindy, a hundred miles away in Herefordshire. Mindy, in turn, had responded to an earlier phone call from me during which I had vomited twice. The vomiting had done the trick and communicated to Mindy the explosive nature of my current intestinal state – my further pleas and callings upon God to spare me his wrath and untie my ruined intestines had served only to confirm to Mindy that, despite whatever lay at the root of my stomach upset, it was business as usual in the Hammond brain and that I wasn't about to die, but would continue moaning for some time and probably needed a doctor.

One had been called and now, a few minutes after first crossing the threshold and introducing himself, we were to be found on the bathroom floor in a moment of medical delicacy perhaps worthy of, but certainly not likely to be featured in, an episode of *ER*. His investigations complete, the kindly doctor made his diagnosis and packed his doctor's bag. I am delighted that they still carry them. Though rather than a comforting, brown leather Gladstone bag bearing the creases and wear of a thousand successful mercy missions, perhaps to wounded sheep farmers in snow-locked bothies or strong yet vulnerable women wrestling in the throes of a difficult labour, the modern doctor's bag tends to be a naff plastic executive briefcase from the eighties that looks more likely to disgorge a Parker pen and a massive mobile phone than a thermometer and a bottle of something with a cork stopper. Which rather undermines the comforting effect of the arrival of said doctor's bag in the hands of a competent, calm and well-trained man or woman with a stethoscope round his or her neck and sensible shoes.

And while on the subject of doctor's styling, why do so many insist on integrating into their otherwise entirely appropriate and conservative outfit a single item of brightly coloured or unnecessarily patterned decoration? It might be a pair of yellow socks, a Mickey Mouse tie or red trousers, but there is always something, just one little detail wilfully woven into their otherwise comfortingly utilitarian and practical clobber with which they hope, I can only guess, to demonstrate to the world that, despite their eminently sensible and responsible job, they are just a little bit whacky. Bet they're great fun at barbecues. I don't object to the family holiday snaps on the desk, or the wall calendar featuring their kids, but, please, spare us

Mongol horseman –
short bloke, long bow.

Horn on the inside, tendon on the outside, the carbon fibre of its day.

'. . . master of horse, bow and terror.'

First time in Hawaii – I didn't need my
swimming trunks

The W M Keck Observatory at Mauna Kea, Hawaii. No, they don't use it to check out the totty on the beach below. At least not when we were there.

Too much sun – I was expecting beach bars and factor 50.

Trust me, this is more exciting than it looks.

I was OK until I tried to turn the beast…

the comedy braces and the flamboyant handkerchief. No item of clothing has ever, ever been funny in its own right, with the single and notable exception of the pith helmet. This is *always*, regardless of wearer or context, funny. Put one on a hat stand in an empty room and I will still laugh at it. So perhaps, then, doctors desirous of demonstrating their edgy, alternative outlook and bubbling sense of humour might like to pitch up to the surgery in a pith helmet. I for one would be immensely cheered by the sight, regardless of the diagnosis coming from underneath it.

The doctor currently packing the tools of his trade into his plastic attaché case was not, however, wearing a pith helmet. And on this particular day even if he had been I would not have been remotely cheered by it as I lay on the floor and fought back another wave of nausea that threatened to send my kidneys up and out at any second, smashing through my clenched teeth like a ram raider. I pressed my cheek into the cool floor tiles and listened for the click of the door as the doctor let himself out. Moving slowly, scared of yet another eruption sending me ricocheting backwards into the hand basin, I rose to stand up and felt the blood drain down to my feet until I felt obliged to check in the mirror that I wasn't entirely transparent. I made the few steps from the bathroom to the living room and swayed in the doorway, hand clenching the doorframe and knees threatening to buckle.

'So what did he say? You look like shit, by the way.' Nick, my brother, was staying at the flat. It was convenient for him with an early start at the office the following morning, though doubtless made significantly less so for having to sit through an evening of listening to me shouting my lunch up on the other side of the paper-thin walls.

'Appendicitis. Gotta have it out tomorrow.' I spoke in bursts, keeping my hand close to my mouth in a protective but futile gesture that could no more have held back the torrent, should it decide to arrive, than Canute could hold back the tide. I talked Nick through the doctor's examination, trying to move swiftly through the less tasteful bits but, inevitably, sparing few details.

'He did *what*? Well, how does that help with the belly-ache? What's he gonna learn by jabbing his finger up there?' He furrowed his brow in mock concentration, mimed the terrible act and then ran a hand through his slicked-back blond hair. 'Takes your mind off it I guess.' He was lounging on the brown leather sofa, suit jacket thrown over the back, legs crossed, tie loosened, cigarette lit. He took a long drag.

'Did he keep the other hand on your shoulder?'

'Furgh offff,' I swayed as another bout off nausea slopped about in my bilges. I took a slow, shaky breath and filled him in on the doctor's diagnosis and his referral of my case to a hospital in the morning. He hadn't wanted to send me in right away as he felt I would be better for trying to get a few hour's sleep, and it would give him a chance to get everything sorted at the hospital before I popped over in the morning to have the cause of my discomfort scissored out.

'Righto. Good luck.' Nick left a pause, during which

he poured a sizeable Scotch. 'You get his number then, or did you give him yours?'

'Oh bugger off,' I clamped my hand to my mouth and grinned despite the misery and sickness. I could see that this could run and run with Nick. He likes a laugh and this was, I had to admit, a big one for him.

'Never mind, mate. Maybe he'll call tomorrow.'

＊

The length of the night – a couple of years at least – and the depth of the misery – deeper than hell – were not brought about solely by the pain in my guts. This was the first time my body had let me down without my having done anything to cause it to fail. Accidents are one thing; you do something daft, you can expect to pay the price every now and then – this theory obviously resonates especially with me. Hangovers are the same – they are something brought upon yourself – a drinking accident, nothing more, and entirely blameless. But this was different altogether. I had not done anything to bring this on myself; it had just decided to happen. And it could be down to only one thing: age.

I am approaching forty. And the use of that phrase is, in itself, revealing enough. Nobody 'approaches' any other age: you either are or are not at that specific age. I didn't 'approach' twenty-one, I just got up one day, realised I was twenty-one and got drunk to celebrate. I may have been sick on my best mate's mum too and lost my watch, but the point is I didn't waste time sneaking up on twenty-one; it just happened. I was twenty, then I was twenty-one, then I was drunk. The end. And nobody has ever 'approached' ten or thirty or ninety-eight. You're either nine or you're ten or you're ninety-eight – well, you're probably dead, but the point is you weren't messing about 'approaching' ninety-eight at the time; you were just pootling about being generally old, forgetting your trousers and goosing the nurses and then you breathed your last. But we 'approach' forty with all the stealth and nervous apprehension that the word can possibly muster. And, frankly, I would rather 'approach' a cornered tiger than 'approach' forty.

I'm not saying that it's been on my mind a lot lately – merely occupied my every waking thought, informed my every action and stalked my dreamscape like a jealous ghost. It just sounds so serious, so sensible, so grown up. And, yes, I know that people over forty can still do daft stuff and that people can still get drunk, go to parties, wear outrageous clothes, drive sports cars, have affairs, wear earrings and change their hair at forty. Of course people do these things; it's practically obligatory. It's called having a mid-life crisis. Sports cars are not bought exclusively by forty-year-old men just because they are the only ones who can afford to insure one; they are bought by forty-year-old men because they are the only ones who need them. And this is not the sort of need that can be ignored or passed over in favour of something else. It can't be equated with the need for fripperies like air or water or heat. This is a need far deeper, far more pressing, that calls from cold, unfathomable depths to the male psyche with all the dreaded attraction and baleful irre-sistibility of the most determined of sirens perched on the most jagged of black rocks.

And men – for it is to men only that the mid-life crisis calls – obey that call in their millions every year. Ask any Ferrari, Porsche or Ray-Ban salesperson about their average customer and you will likely hear that he is not, as the adverts would have us believe, a virile young footballer with shiny hair, a rippling six pack and a trouser pouch like a new punch bag. He is, in fact, a middle-aged bloke wearing more chins than he started life with and carrying the clear evidence of forty years of beer and pies slung across his midriff. The watch, the earring, the shoes and the teeth are expensive and suggestive of potency, power and speed. The bearer of them, however, might be wealthier than he was, but he is also heavier, slower, saggier and, secretly, a bit more tired than he used to be. And I can say all of these things because I am a thirty-nine-year-old man twirling Ferrari keys and growing my hair again so that I can say I did these things before I was forty anyway, and deny that it is in any way in response to the deep-seated sense that I am past my prime, am seen by the world in a light very different from that in which I see myself and am heading at speed for the big door marked 'out'.

And now, this sudden failure of my appendix to go about the business of doing whatever it is a young, pink appendix does, had plunged me into a cauldron of testos-terone-loaded panic and tummy ache. I lay awake through the small hours – never understood that: they're bloody massive hours at the time, each one lasting a day or so – and pondered this first sign of the gradual but inevitable failure of my middle-aged body. Presumably my eyes will go next, forcing me to adopt those bloody terrible reading specs bought from petrol stations and apparently paraded just for fun and hilarity by middle-aged men when confronted with a menu or a speeding ticket but that in fact prove to be an absolute necessity if their poor, myopic peepers are to determine anything smaller than a dining table or closer to their newly hair-packed nose than the other side of the room.

I wondered how it feels the first time you emerge from the gents and glance down to see that ominous dark coin of shame spread across the front of your Chinos which tells the world that, yes, you are indeed a middle-aged man and can't be relied upon entirely to finish anything you are saying or doing in a neat and prompt fashion and might be prone to the odd afterthought. Through the pain and misery, as my malfunctioning appendix swelled up and got ready to go bang, I glimpsed a grim world singularly suited to my current state but for which I could generate not a jot of enthusiasm any more than I might for leaping into a giant blender or becoming a Member of Parliament. I'll be honest: I thought of how I might welcome death's cold embrace and beg her to take me into her frosty bosom and cart me off before things became undignified. And then I was sick again, so the whole dignity thing went out of the window and I slept on the bathroom floor with a patch of sick dried to my chin and wearing one sock.

Morning came – they always do – and I said goodbye to

Nick as he strode off, all sharply-tailored suit, posh pen and expensive shoes, along the banks of the Thames to hop on the high-speed boat to his important, responsible, glamorous and ever-so-slightly cool job. I padded around the flat in my sock, considered being sick again, managed not to be and pulled on my favourite jeans and a brown T-shirt with Ducati written on it. I don't actually own a Ducati any more, and so, technically, the wearing of a T-shirt bearing the company name and logo renders me viable for immediate and painful execution. But I really didn't care that morning and it was the first thing to come to hand when I opened the wardrobe and surveyed a tangle of cowboy boots, crumpled dinner suits and boxer shorts. Our little London flat is very much a functional, practical thing; it's not a place I consider or ever want to consider home. Home is the place where I live with Mindy and the girls. The flat is a place I stay when I am working and cannot get home. I don't wish to feel too comfortable and 'at home' there and so I keep the décor low-key and impersonal. It is, in short, a shithole; a fact pointed out by Mindy on the rare occasion she joins me there on a weekday night. It is kitted out to conform, with unnerving accuracy, to the student house aesthetic. That is to say, the washing machine is knackered, and although there is actually quite a posh cooker with a metal extractor hood, it has never, ever, been used and the cupboard space is dedicated primarily to housing beer, tins of soup and more beer.

But food was not on my mind that morning; there was, as it happened, quite a lot of food on my bathroom floor, but that was the remnants of the previous evening's discomforts and not something to be considered or dealt with right now.

In the event, the business of removing a faulty appendix was rather more of a bother for the blokes doing it than it was for me. All that was required of me, as the patient, was to take a nice lie-down while wearing a nightie that did up at the back and wake up again feeling woozy and pleasant. Mindy had done the nervous relative bit, talking to me and holding my hand as I zonked out under the anaesthetic. Thinking about it afterwards, I realised that it had probably served for her as a rather unpleasant reminder of my previous times in hospital. Naturally, though, I didn't think of this at the time and ploughed on merrily in the belief that the grief and stress were all mine and that I was being really very brave in coping with it all. Still being brave, I wafted along in a state of half-consciousness, quite enjoying the attention as nurses and orderlies pottered about me, asking after my comfort and telling me that all had gone well in theatre and I would soon be up on my feet. As my head cleared, I looked around and took in the small room they had wheeled me into. On the bedside table I saw my watch and reading book. This, then, was where I had started off earlier in the day, trying to laugh with Mindy when I came out of the bathroom with my white arse hanging out of the back of the nightie and got into bed ready for collection by the orderlies.

The surgeon himself made an appearance in my room.

'Right then, Richard, we removed your appendix and, from the state of it, I'd say you've had two or three bouts of appendicitis in the past.'

'Yeah, well, I maybe noticed a bit of a bellyache a couple of times,' I told him, and tried to look like the kind of tough guy who could shrug off a bout of appendicitis as nothing more than a sore tummy – a tricky look to carry off while wearing a nightie with blue flowers on it, but I'm pretty sure I managed it. In fact, I was sure I had suffered precisely two bouts before because I could remember being in a lot of pain and growing quickly exhausted from the effort of moaning to Mindy about it on two previous occasions.

'Guess some people don't feel it so bad.' I exhaled casually as I spoke and raised a manly eyebrow.

'Yes. Very good. Now, we fixed your hernia for you on the way out, too.' The specialist consulted notes as he spoke, glancing back up at me with a confident smile.

I sat up. Which hurt a bit.

'My what?' I didn't have a hernia, couldn't have. I would have noticed. The doctor carried on.

'And we carried out a couple of scans as well. Looks like you've got a kidney stone there.'

The doctor showed me a printout from a scan, waving the paper at me, but my head was doing the swimmy thing and I couldn't concentrate on it.

'A what? Hernia stone, kidney scan? I didn't know about any of these, I er …'

The doctor, having delivered his news, smiled benignly, turned and left the room.

So this was it then, the beginning of the end. My innards were clearly dissolving by the hour, my eyes would pack up soon, and my ears and no doubt my family jewels shrivel up and drop off like a scab. I lifted the bedclothes gingerly, suddenly keen to check all was well in the undercarriage department and also to inspect whatever scar I might have been left with following my operation of just an hour or so earlier. Under the sheets, I peeled the nightie up and off to the side and saw a large medical dressing covering my lower belly. This, then, was where the surgeon had 'gone in'. I recalled the specialist telling me that he would be operating via my belly button and that any scarring would be contained very tightly within that area. I had responded breezily that I really didn't mind a scar or two; it was inevitable that a body should show signs of wear and tear.

Secretly, I was very keen to be left with a scar, largely because recent escapades in my life, while leaving mental scars deeper than canyons, have failed to leave a single physical mark on me. A source of constant disappointment, especially when in the company of chaps comparing scars – as they will, trust me; they just do – and in the face of a myriad manly gashes from rugby studs, speedboat props and shark's teeth, I am forced to concede that my only actual scar is a small nick on my left hand where I ran it down a wall as a kid and failed to spot the nail head protruding from the heavily patterned wallpaper in time to stop it gouging a slice out of the fleshy bit of my thumb. You see, I can't even make it sound remotely exciting here, so what chance in a pub full of drunken blokes suddenly all bearing more scars than a load of bloody Vikings?

Something about the medical dressing stuck to my gut caught my attention and stopped my reverie. The thick, white pad went very low, very low indeed. Almost into my … Holy shit, it should have barged down into the dense and manly forest of fur gathered around the sloping foothills of my belly. It should, in short, have been stuck to my pubes. But it wasn't because the doctors had clearly taken the precaution of engaging in some pre-emptive deforestation down there prior to the operation. They had shaved half my bloody pubes off. I couldn't help emitting a quiet and disappointingly high squeak as I snatched the covers back further and bent almost double to inspect the horror. Worse, they didn't appear to have shaved the area after all but had, instead, deployed rusty garden shears to carry out an act of topiary so shabby and imprecise that I was left briefly confused as to whether I should contact the Medical Council or *Gardeners' Question Time*.

'Yes, lady there in the blue cardie …'

'Mabel Northrop from the Accrington Amateur Gardeners' Group, my husband's pubic hedge is a not doing at all well, it's all patchy and uneven, the doctors tried trimming it but they made it worse, some bits tall and thick, others as bald as his head. Whatever should I do …'

'I'd sue the buggers for negligence, Mabel. And plant yew instead; takes a while to grow but wonderful once it's established.'

It was the edging that let it down, I decided. No attempt had been made to trim neatly or in any sort of straight line or regular curve. I am told that some chaps trim their nether regions for aesthetic reasons, and, while I can't quite see the point of that – I mean, it's not the most aesthetically appealing of areas, even to those for whom it holds all sorts of promise, and trimming the setting seems to me to be as pointless as mowing the lawns at an abbatoir. I risked another look at the devastation.

Yes, it would grow back, I knew that, but, really, I would prefer the doctor to have stuck to cutting holes and removing things, doing the heavy labour and structural work rather than carrying out the medical equivalent of tweaking the soft furnishings. I dropped the covers back down to cover the whole sorry scene and sank back on to the pillows to stare up at the rough polystyrene ceiling tiles. Unbidden and unwelcome, Sinatra's song floated into my head: 'And now, the end is near …' I half smiled at the horror of it all and sank into drug-addled sleep, one hand draped protectively across my vegetable patch. This would not be my last hospital stay of the year and it is unlikely that I would have taken much solace from the knowledge that things would get much worse before they ever got better. In my dreams I ran through fields as a ten-year-old boy, trailing a stick and shouting into the wind and forty was far, far over the horizon. But it was waiting there.

The Procedure

'No, Richard, it's an actual drill, a proper drill that, y'know, drrrrrrrrr,' and the doctor, an elegant man in his mid-forties with an expensive tan and the blackest hair I have ever seen, mimed the action of a hand drill to make his point. He stood in front of his desk while I sat on a smoothly finished wooden chair in the centre of his consulting room. The thin carpet was dark blue under my cowboy boots and the walls the palest cream. Everything was smart, clean and quite expensive. The wall calendar displayed an Aston Martin and a laurel bush above the month, June.

I had elected to investigate having this kidney stone nuked privately so that I might fit its destruction in with my diary. This was Harley Street. I kept turning the phrase over in my mind, 'Harley Street'. On arriving, earlier in the day, I had expected it to be full of Victorian gents in stovepipe hats striding purposefully amongst carriages with lanterns on the front and shouting at children playing with metal hoops and sticks. It wasn't, of course; it turned out to be another busy, London street, with expensive cars filling the parking spaces outside the many establishments set up for the removal of people's kidney stones, in-growing toenails, and money.

Up here, in the consulting room where, presumably, hundreds of the wealthy and powerful had sat to be informed of the progress of their gout, their blocked arteries, swollen joints and shrivelling bank accounts, the doctor was still explaining to me the process by which he would reduce my kidney stone to powder with a proper electric drill that went 'drrrrrr'. I tuned in, as far as I could, to his soft, smooth tones and watched in fascination as his imaginary drill chewed its way through at least a foot of imaginary wall. It appeared to be on 'hammer' setting and I began to feel sorry for the stone.

'And you don't even have to cut me open, right?' I asked the question without lifting my eyes from the good doctor's clean hands, still gripping the invisible handle of his imaginary drill. He wore a wedding ring and on his desk a photograph of beautiful wife and children shone quietly from within a sturdy, lacquered frame. Good signs these in a doctor, I figured. He was a married man, a family man, someone who understood stuff. In the photograph, his beautiful wife showed amazing white teeth in a broad grin. She had dark hair, deep brown eyes and wore a floppy straw sun hat with an orange flower resting on its brim. I tried not to let my gaze roam anywhere inappropriate around her green bikini. Quite well off, doctors, and nearly always married to glamorous women, I'd noticed. Or do they get their family photographs from some sort of mail order company set up to provide medical practitioners with all the paraphernalia necessary to reassure their patients that they are, in fact, steady, respectable members of society and not adrenaline-fuelled thrill monkeys whose holidays are spent paragliding and learning to pole dance?

I was just taking in the finer points of the velvety curves of his wife, or perhaps the model, in his family photograph, when my wandering eyes, and mind, were snapped smartly back to reality by the doctor's utterance of the word 'penis'. I focussed again on what he was saying, probably frowning with the effort.

'And then from there, up the narrow tube, called the ureter, to the kidney. We find the stone, hit it with the drill', he did the mime again, leaning his shoulder forwards and bracing himself against the recoil from the spinning tip as it bit into my kidney stone. 'Then we pull out the drill and send in a wire with a manipulator and bag on the end, gather up all the bits and pull 'em out. Job done.' He smiled an expensively even smile and clasped his sturdy, manicured hands together, having put the imaginary drill down in order to mime the act of gathering the shards of ruined kidney stone with some sort of remote-control grab inside, presumably, my kidney. I was still wondering about the penis bit of all this.

'Sorry, just to backtrack a bit, you, er, you go in through, er …'

'The penis, in through there,' he began another mime, this one too awful to contemplate as his hands described the twists and turns involved in hauling a piece of DIY equipment up through my most sensitive parts and along a route more tortuous by far than that faced by Hannibal as he made his way, complete with tool belt and pencil behind ear, through my bladder and out the other side, finishing inside my kidney with, I imagined, a cup of tea and a quick sit-down before setting his shoulder to the drill and getting on with the heavy stuff in there.

'What, so you take an actual drill in?' I performed a brief mime of my own, pointing in as delicate a manner as possible to my crotch.

'Yes, it's a drill, an actual drill that goes drrrrr.'

'Yes, I get that bit, it's a real drill, but here's the thing; you go in there and then all the way,' I wound my hands around my midriff in a manner probably not entirely faithful to the medical realities of what lay inside but by which I hoped to sort of generally indicate the complexities of the journey ahead of the man and his apparently quite expansive toolbox.

'Yes, through the bladder, up through the ureter — yours is quite narrow and a bit kinked, by the way, which explains why you've suffered with a stone so much in the past — and then into your kidney.'

'Yes, but,' I decided to ignore this obvious slight on my ureter and to press my point home, 'but you start,' more pointing, this time slowly and with, I don't mind admitting, a shaking hand, 'here.'

And the doctor explained that, by starting his journey in this manner, he avoided the need to cut me open and carve a doorway of his own, relying instead on what Mother Nature had, albeit perhaps not intentionally, provided. It took some digesting, this particular piece of news. I was due to undergo what would from now on, I gathered, be called 'The Procedure' in just a week's time. That meant I had a week to prepare. I couldn't think how. Clearly, I wasn't about to wander off to the workshop at home, reach for the Black and Decker and set to getting the old system ready for what was shortly to happen. Instead, I vowed to try and forget about it.

I was in the middle of preparing to shoot a pilot for what could potentially be a large-scale studio show for the BBC. Actually, the thing would turn out not to be required at the present time and it never did see the light of day. But you don't make advances in technical and creative fields like television without experimenting and trying new things. We might, for all we knew at that stage, have been working on the new *Generation Game* or the new *Doctor Who*. Whatever, there were meetings with execs to be sat through, discussions about stage sets, contributors and editorial content to be considered. The director of photography had to decide how many cameras we would need and where to put them, the lighting director had to consider how to light the studio and in what colours for best effect, given the timbre of the show and the audience expectations. I had to decide what jacket to wear.

There was, in short, much to be done. And the more the merrier as far as I was concerned. I felt that I should leave this doctor's consulting room at once in search of as many facts, deadlines, pressing issues and complicated ideas as I could find in order to fill my mind and force from it any thoughts of the impending operation during which a man, and presumably a team of supporters, would get tooled up with drills, special grabs and bags and set off en masse for my kidney using a route that began with them approaching my … I had to get out quite urgently now and rose to make the fact obvious.

'Right, so we're all booked in then. I'll bring something to read and, er, that'll be that then. Right. Thanks, doctor. Look forward to it. Well, not look forward obviously, but …' I extended a hand to shake his, my mind instantly straying back to the imaginary drill so recently grasped in the large appendage now held in my own. I wanted to ask again, just to clarify, that it was a real drill, one using kinetic energy and not sonic power or something a bit more impressive and space age. But I figured this was a can of worms best forced shut until I absolutely had to face the contents.

The meetings to make final arrangements and preparations for my pilot show proved a welcome, if not entirely successful, distraction. I discovered that, even in the midst of the most heartfelt and impassioned debate with senior BBC types about where this planned show was going, to whom it might appeal and how it might be considered in the BBC's overarching responsibilities to the licence fee-paying public, the prospect of my forthcoming operation rather interfered with my ability to focus on the matter under discussion. While the execs drank earnest tea, peered over their designer glasses and discussed the need for openness, honesty and a grounded approach to contributors in the unavoidably fantasy-tinged arena of a television studio, I gazed into the middle distance and, in my mind's eye, watched as a fleet of tiny medical men with white beards and pointy hats set off towards my John Thomas with picks over their shoulders singing 'Hi ho, hi ho, it's up your knob we go', in tiny but strangely sinister squeaky voices. It was quite a long week. At the end of it, a date was set for the studio recording and for a filming trip to a village on the north-east coast of England where I would carry out undercover filming operations in a chip shop. It was all very exciting and exactly the sort of thing I'd dreamed of doing when I was at college, twenty years earlier. And not a single scrap of it lodged in my mind because it was taken up, all of it, by one giant thought, squatting there like a massive, bloated cuckoo chick in a nest now bereft of its original, smaller and altogether more wholesome incumbents. Tomorrow was the day. 'The Procedure' would begin at 3.30 p.m. and finish, well, finish sometime after they'd, well, after they'd done all that they needed to do. It was no big deal, of course not. People undergo far, far more intensive, painful, scary and downright risky procedures every day and they do so with dignity and grace. I determined to do the same.

'Mindy,' I shouted down the stairs, 'will they put me in that nightie again or do I need to take in some pyjamas?' I tried to keep my tone light and confident. But the words came out sounding strangled and nervous. I was packing, ready for the overnight stay that would follow 'The Procedure'.

'They'll put you in a nightie again, you pillock,' Mindy shouted up from the kitchen, busy preparing tea for the girls. I don't actually own any pyjamas, but it had seemed an appropriate enquiry to make.

'Righto.' I struggled to keep my mood up and stuffed a toothbrush, razor, shaving foam and socks into a small suitcase. The few homely things rattled around the bottom of it.

'And don't forget some nice pants.' Mindy had come to the bottom of the stairs to shout to me in the bedroom and I imagined her gripping the banister and grinning up at the landing.

'Yes, right, thank you.' I tried to smile, pulling my face as taut as I could but failing. I felt my cheeks hang like the sides of a badly pitched tent. And I stuffed a pair of shreddies into the suitcase. Even with a book added, a tube of toothpaste and a magazine about motorcycles, the little suitcase was still half empty and when I shut the lid and tilted it upright to grasp the handle, the contents slid down and rattled into a pile at the bottom. It sounded kind of hopeless, like a set of intestines no longer supported by young, taut, fleshy membranes, but loose and hanging limp and grey into the tired cavity below. And I imagined a similar scene being played out inside my ageing carcass. I was not in an especially buoyant mood, if I'm honest, and it was rather colouring my outlook. The whole hitting forty thing was hanging over my head like a grand piano on a fraying wire. In my darker moments, I had actually found it a consolation to consider that my almost certain demise under the knife would at least mean that I would be spared the misery of passing forty and prolonging the whole business.

And then I had recalled that I wouldn't, in fact, be under the knife at all, rather that the entire affair, surgeons, tools and essential supplies, would set off to travel along the interior of my most personal portions like a team of miners carrying tool boxes, lanterns and canaries in cages. It's a strange thing, but I have noticed that my imagination, while reasonably robust and capable of playing the occasional blinder when called upon to do so for work or entertainment, really only rolls up its sleeves and gets cracking properly when my mind is at its most vulnerable, when I am feeling low, scared, nervous or just in need of a good night's sleep freed from hordes of terrifying creatures and panting supermodels invading my head. The nights of late had been long and tortuous, full of variously startling dreams, the sharing of which with another mortal soul might have attracted the attention of a psychologist. Or, in the darkest depths of one or two of the nights, the police. I was feeling, then, not at my sparkly best as I lugged the rattling suitcase down the stairs, reflecting with every step how closely the tumbling, jumbling collection of artefacts within the case mimicked the loose, disparate and largely broken assemblage rolling around inside me now.

'Right, well, I'm ready for the off, then. Here we go.' I tried to make it sound like the sort of motivational launch holler my parents would give as we pulled away on a camping holiday in our Austin Allegro estate. It sounded pathetic and Mindy looked up.

'You all right?'

'Yes. Fine. It'll all be okay. Just a man climbing up me todger with a drill in his hand. Nothing to worry about. You've had two babies and you never made a fuss. Well … you did go on a bit, but I gather it does smart, so I completely understood …' and I looked into Mindy's face and grinned. I felt better immediately.

'Yes, all right. I hope he wears really big boots and snags his drill bit on the sides.'

'Oomph.' I winced and crossed my legs, stuffing my hand into my groin and blowing out my cheeks in mock reaction. It would all be fine. Mindy smiled and took a step towards me, gripping me in a hug.

᛭

It wasn't the slipping under the anaesthetic that bothered me most; rather, it was the slipping out of it at the other end of the whole business that brought with it distress. The lady had come up to my room to find me lying beneath the covers, sheet pulled up to my nose, ready for the off.

'Ah, so this is it, then. I'm, er, ready. What do we do? I haven't eaten all day, honest. Not even a glass of water for hours now. I'm parched, huh, could kill a beer. Not that I drink to excess, you understand. Bet you're tired of hearing that. How long's it going to take?' I talk a lot when I'm nervous.

Mindy sat in the corner of my room, watching as the nurse asked me to slip an arm out from under the covers so that she could check my blood pressure for the thousandth time since I had arrived barely two hours before. I sat up, ready to transfer across to a wheelchair or walk to a lift. Or do anything, really, as long as it was something that could be done while wearing a nightie. This one was slightly better than the last; it featured a dense, geometric pattern in a mid-shade of green against a lighter green background. You wouldn't choose it for your prom night, but it had the edge on the blue flowery number at the last place, for sure.

The nurse made it clear to me that I was simply to lie back on the bed while she and a keen young orderly with sideburns, who had arrived in the room looking ready for a mountain bike race, pushed the bed out through the door, along a corridor and into a lift. She then made it equally clear to Mindy, following our progress between the potted plants and literature stands, that this was as far as she went. Realising that this was it, the parting of the ways, the end of the line, Mindy and I did all the touching of hands stuff, said we loved each other and promised to be back soon. And then we parted, Mindy stepping back to allow the dull grey doors of the lift to close.

'Okay, so, on my own from here on, then. Apart from you two, obviously.' I watched the faces of the nurse and the orderly with the sideburns in the mirrored lift walls. 'And the doctor, obviously.' Neither of them smiled in any meaningful way, but the orderly raised an eyebrow in what might have been acknowledgement. 'Well, at least he'd better show up. Otherwise it'll all be a bit of an anticlimax, getting all dressed up like this and everything.' I laughed, nervously. The lift landed at our floor and they wheeled me out in silence.

It's theatrical, the business of entering an operating theatre. With you, as the patient, there not to watch but to be part of the show – the main attraction, in fact. I was wheeled into a sort of anteroom, where a woman with big arms and a surgical smock one size too small, prepared me for the anaesthetic. We chatted about stuff, about the weather, about the room we were in and eventually, even about The Procedure that would begin as soon as my unconscious body was wheeled through the curtains and under the lights to take centre stage. Still unsure, even earlier that morning, as to whether The

Procedure would be taking place under local or general anaesthetic, I had prepared a killer line, ready for deployment when the moment came. I would look the doctor in the eye, managing to appear steely and tough, even in a nightie, and tell him that he faced a straight choice today. 'On the subject of anaesthetic,' I would say, in dry, quiet tones that didn't actually belong to me but that I would somehow appropriate for the moment and use, 'you've got a choice. You come at my tackle with that thing', and I would pat my manly bulge beneath the nightie and then point dismissively at his power drill, 'and one of us is going to be unconscious. You decide.' Clint Eastwood moment, pure theatre. 'You, or me.'

In the event, I said something to the anaesthetist about how much I loved my children and passed out. At least, I must have passed out because seemingly only seconds later I was aware of waking up. It was over. 'The Procedure' had taken place and this, presumably, was not heaven. But while the passing out had really not been so bad – apart from my failure to deliver my killer line – the coming to had rather less pleasant ramifications. For one thing, I was horribly disoriented – as is common, apparently, in such circumstances. For another, though, as I took in where I was, what had happened, all that sort of thing, I became aware that I was back in the anteroom where the anaesthetist had chatted away before knocking me out more surely than a prize fighter. But I was not alone. I was very much not alone, in fact. A horde of types in medical garb hovered around me. Most were female. All were busy and all, clearly, were involved in 'The

Procedure' in one way or another.

'Wow,' my voice worked, though it was quiet and dry; rather as I had intended it to be for the killer line I never actually delivered. 'Were all of you …' I attempted a nod back in the direction of the theatre, 'y'know, in there for, er, *it*?'

A general murmuring confirmed that, yes, they had been. And a little cache of memory slammed back into my head in a single burst. As I slipped into unconsciousness, dutifully counting backwards from ten, my knees had been raised up and apart, the better to allow access to the portal through which the good doctor and his minions would soon be working. I swivelled my eyes around to try and take in the scene as I lay on my hospital bed with a drip in my arm and a worrying breeze blowing up my nightie. There seemed to be about fifteen people in the room; all wearing medical garb and all, with just one exception, female.

'Did it really need so many?' I wheezed quietly. No one answered, no doubt unable to hear my straining voice over the brisk and efficient clatter of medical paraphernalia being packed away. It felt, suddenly, rather like being one of the stragglers at some form of uncommonly clean and ordered student party, still asleep with his head in the fireplace while the residents cleared up the equivalent of empty beer bottles, pizza boxes and polystyrene cups with warm wine and fag ends in them. In one way, it was rather pleasant to consider oneself as having been the centre of attention for so many bright young things. They had trained for years in order to pursue their vocation, these people. They were able to heal the sick, to mend bones and remove kidney stones. They were young, clever, glamorous, generous-spirited by definition, technically capable and very much the hope for this nation's future. And they had all seen my willy. All of them.

God, the thought slammed into my head like a freight train into the buffers; one of them, perhaps her with the stethoscope and the pens in her pocket, or maybe her with the fitted smock and the dark curls cascading from under her hat like a shampoo advert, must have been the surgeon's closest assistant. The good doctor, though dexterous to a fault and as nimble-fingered as the most artful and creative seamstress, could not possibly have both carried out the operation itself, manipulating the drill, the grab and so forth and at the same time supported the means by which his medical machinery was gaining access to the field of battle. It followed, therefore, that his assistant must have carried out that role for him. That is to say, one of these women fluttering about me now in a cloud of clean scent and washed hair must have spent the past hour or so gripping my willy while a doctor fed a drill up it, smashed a small boulder to pieces and fetched the bits out in a bag.

I pondered the indignity that had been visited on my person by the nature of 'The Procedure'. And I prayed that no one, at least, would mention *Top Gear* and thus personalise the whole experience by making clear their awareness of the connection between the bouncy, chatty individual familiar from the telly and the sweaty, pasty-faced, soon-to-be-middle-aged person in a nightie with his knees in the air and his knob out.

'I love *Top Gear*, by the way,' a blue-eyed nurse with the look of a rabbit in a chocolate commercial confided as she breezed past in a cloud of crisp, starched air.

'Shit.' And I slumped back into the pillows, welcoming once more the oncoming wave that signified unconsciousness. They will have seen my badly-edged lawn, too, I told myself, miserably recalling the tatty edging surrounding whatever now lay in ruins beneath the thin folds of my hospital nightie. And in my dreams I headed back for the fields, desperate to be that ten-year-old boy with the stick again.

*

'Sleep well?'

An innocent enough enquiry but one lucky not to be met with a carefully aimed cowboy boot.

'Yup, fine thank you, doctor.' I hadn't, of course, but found myself slipping back into that defensive mode in which hospital patients will do anything at all to convince their jailers that they are fit, well and would benefit most of all from being released back into nature to fend for themselves. The doctor ran a finger almost longingly along the bracket holding up my reading lamp. He was thin, grey-haired and had a narrow, lined face that looked as if it might have been stretched at some point. And he was clearly proud of this and all the other rooms in the private Harley Street hospital from which and in which he operated.

'Everything to your liking? The food? All this?' And he made a grand gesture across the cramped, hot room with his arm as though trying to take in the Mongolian steppe, the plains of Africa and the drifting sands of the Empty Quarter in one sweep.

'Yes. Fine, thanks.' I rather wished this customer satisfaction survey would hurry up and finish, for two reasons. Firstly, I wanted to get the heck out of Dodge and go home. Secondly, I was painfully aware that my night recuperating in a private hospital from a minor kidney procedure had cost me, ironically enough, about the same as an entire, new kidney on the black market and I wanted to turn my back on the place as soon as possible and have a damned good shout about it.

'Well, you should be fine to leave today, your blood pressure's fine, your temperature's fine, you're ...'

'Fine?' I ventured.

'Yup. Fine.' He gave me a thin-lipped smile and clasped his hands together.

'Anyone you need to call about being picked up?'

'Wife's on the way.'

'Good, good. Fine. Now, just a couple of things, then.' And he delivered a lecture on how, after blasting the kidney stone to dust with the drill, the surgeon had carefully removed all traces of it and then, via the same dreaded portal as that through which he had removed the rubble, had inserted a special tube that connected my kidney to my bladder. Called a stent, this was a temporary fixture that would be left in place for a few weeks to give everything a chance to sort of settle down after being disrupted and, medically speaking, pissed off by all the crowds.

'Now, in some cases, the patient can reject the stent …'

'What, wrong colour?'

He looked confused.

'Clashes with his pyjamas?'

'Erm,' he looked entirely at sea now and reached up to his pocket for a pen.

'I'm joking. It's okay.'

'Fine, fine. No, the patient's body can reject the stent.'

'What, sort of spit it out in disgust?'

'Well, kind of. It's most unusual, though, but if you get any trouble, any discomfort, just call us and we can whisk you back in and remove it.' He tapped the pen thoughtfully against his fingertips.

I really didn't want to ask how it would be removed. I could guess. And I certainly didn't want to think about how much it would cost. I vowed that the thing could eat its way out of my insides on its own before I would submit my body and my wallet to any further indignities. The stent, lying limp and lifeless deep within my innards, must have caught this thought and decided to see if it couldn't do exactly that.

*

'Yeah, the thing is, though,' and I watched the back of the driver's ears carefully for a sign that he was really going to take in what I was about to tell him, 'they don't cut you open, they go in via your old fella.' I finished with a note of satisfaction I couldn't quite keep out of my voice and waited for my words to take effect. They did. I watched as James, the driver provided by the BBC in consideration of my fragile state, to transport me to an east coast seaside town for the purpose of making a film for my forthcoming – but sadly doomed – studio pilot, squirmed in his seat in front of me.

'What, your …?'

'Oh yes, they stick a pipe up there, all the way through your bladder to your kidney, then poke a drill up it, blast the stone and then haul the bits out through the same way they went in.'

In the three days since my return home following The Procedure, I had found that the story of what was done to me in Harley Street got better and better with the telling. I may have embellished here and there, added a little something where I felt it was needed for balance or pace and perhaps talked up the size of the stone itself and of the drill. In certain company, I may have made claims to the effect that I could now pee a grand piano and not feel a thing and that I had woken in theatre, midway through The Procedure, to find the entire female cast of the *Charlie's Angels* remake standing around my bed taking off their glasses and shaking their hair down with amazement at my bravery. But even the pared-back, truthful version I was giving James now could illicit the most tremendous response if you spoke earnestly and sincerely. I watched as a shudder travelled up and down his spine and his ears reddened with the horror of realisation.

'So how are you now?'

'Oh I'm fine. It's like looking down at the end of a

trombone when I pee, obviously, but I'm fine.' I shuffled in the back seat, leaning forwards very slightly to take the weight off my lower back and considered just how 'fine' I really didn't feel.

It was a long journey and we made many stops. The doctors had made very clear to me the importance of drinking a lot of fluids to really flush out my kidney following 'The Procedure'. It was a miserable experience, sitting there and being lectured about my waterworks, but I vowed to follow their advice to the letter.

I apologise for going into such detail here concerning the exact nature of their advice, given the distasteful and sensitive subject to which the advice pertained, but it is important to arm you with the facts if you are to stand a chance of appreciating the dilemma in which I now found myself. The doctor had also warned me that, with the stent in place, linking kidney to bladder, my capacity, as it were, would be reduced. That is to say, I might find myself obliged to pay visits to the throne room a lot more frequently than usual. And they also explained that the end of the stent itself bore several plastic spikes, designed to hold the pipe in place inside the kidney and that these were particularly important when the bladder deflated. I need not, I'm sure, elaborate on why this deflation might occur, suffice it to say that whenever I 'excused' myself, the resulting 'excuse' would result in a reduction in volume of the contents and therefore size of the bladder exactly commensurate with the volume of 'excuses' I made. That is to say, when I had a pee, my bladder would shrink down in size, pulling the stent pipe down, away from the kidney, where it would be held in place only by the spikes in the end of the stent itself.

The doctor had also explained, patiently, and, I am afraid, without even a thousandth the gravitas he would have required to ever effectively communicate the immensity of the pain and horror about to be visited upon my meagre frame, that the spiked end of the stent had, unfortunately, come to rest on the exact same spot in my kidney as was previously occupied by the stone that had brought about the need for 'The Procedure' in the first place. And that site, he had told me, bending forwards now, lowering an eyebrow or two and at last looking like he was trying to put his back into giving me a sense of the drama and the importance of what he was about to share with me, was a bit infected as a result. It might be a bit tender, therefore, when I peed. I might, he told me, feel a bit of discomfort.

Righto. Tender. Only when I peed. That would be okay, I figured, and I dismissed the doctor's doleful warning as something intended for lesser types who couldn't cope with a bit of discomfort. What they were telling me, in fact, was that I needed to drink more than usual, to clear out my kidney and that this would exacerbate a need to pee more than usual because of a reduced bladder capacity and that this would, in turn, make worse the discomfort of the stent that had been fixed, temporarily, inside me until everything following the operation had calmed down a bit. And the stent itself had insisted on settling on the very same spot made sore by the problem, the alleviation of which had given rise to the need for the stent to be there in the first place.

Right, well, the whole circumstance was dripping in irony, I could see that for sure, but I could cope. I was, after all, nearly forty and very much a man of the world. If I couldn't deal with a bit of a sting when I took a pee, then I wasn't the man I thought I was. In the event, I cried like a baby. Shuffling back from the lavatory, crossing the landing and making my way back to our bedroom in the middle of the night with one hand clutching protectively at the pathetic lump in the front of my pyjamas, I sniffed and stared down at my bare feet on the carpet in the dim light. I reached the door and turned the handle to walk into our room, taking tiny steps and stopping every third one to regain my composure. Inside our bedroom, in the dim light of a reading lamp, I saw from the movement of the huddled lump under the duvet that Mindy was awake.

'You okay?' her voice came, muffled, from under the covers. She sounded warm and soft and caring but she might have been a million miles away from me, locked as I was in my twilight world of lonely, degrading pain.

'Yeah.' I sniffed again. Mindy sat up and looked at me with hollow, tired eyes.

'I'm just not ready for trouble with my waterworks yet.' I clutched again at my trousers. 'I mean, I'm forty this year, not bloody eighty. And I'm just not ready for all this', and I waved an arm back outside, indicating the bathroom where I had, only moments earlier, yelped and tried to suppress a full-blooded scream as what seemed to be an explosion of razor blades tore through my kidney when the stent's spike clawed down on to the red-raw site already tortured by the stone.

And so as I sat now, trying to find a comfortable position in the back of the car, I knew that within the next half-hour I would be asking James to pull over at a service station where I would hobble across the forecourt like an old man and then stand at the porcelain like an even older man, wincing and trying not to scream.

While the doctors had indeed been thorough in their issuing of warnings concerning what I should or shouldn't be doing, and what I might or might not expect to occur in the privacy of the smallest room, none of them had suggested or even hinted that what I was about to do that day might be advantageous or therapeutic in any way. As far as I am aware, in fact, no doctor has ever recommended pretending to be a pizza boy, arriving by motorcycle and walking into a snack bar to deliver to the owner an unexpected surprise under the close scrutiny of hidden cameras in the course of making a pilot TV show for the BBC as a means of recuperating from anything. It's rather stressful, actually: there are so many things that can go wrong.

We had the agreement of the chap's wife and family and, it seemed, the compliance of half of the town in which he lived and ran his business. He turned out to be an immensely popular man, one given to spontaneous acts of kindness and generosity and a person to whom the televised presentation of a cheque for several hundred pounds would doubtless provide a spectacle that would galvanise the nation into a mass of satisfaction that someone had got what they genuinely deserved. The show was going to be great, the set-up for the day's filming was great, the cameras were all in their hidden locations and the couple of actors hired to pretend to be customers in his shop while secretly filming on a camera hidden in their holdall were happily chatting, drinking tea and surreptitiously hitting the record button at table number five.

All was well. Except that I needed a pee and knew that, when I went for one, I would be thrown to my knees with the shrieking agony of it. Which is kind of a tricky thing to carry off in a public lavatory without raising comment. Again, I apologise for the personal nature of this tale, but there it is, that's what happened. It is, I'm sure, less of a chore to suffer the discomfort of reading about someone's most personal of functions than ever it is to be the person whose personal functions are causing him to scream bloody murder at every available opportunity and wonder quite what it is you have to do in order to induce a faint and make the pain go away. I don't wish to give the impression that I am a drama queen; I'm really not. It was quite spectacularly painful.

And so, wearing a crash helmet to hide my face and with an earpiece jammed into my left ear so as to relay to me the progress and state of the TV cameras, the chap's wife having helped us hide all around the café, I entered the establishment, confident that my walk, at least, would kill off any glimmer of an idea on the part of the chap that the man standing in front of him holding a pizza box and asking for Mr Whatever in a pained, thin voice was, in fact, the sprightly little fella off that car show. Watching me from the back of the shop, he must have wondered at how fate might have led to an elderly and clearly very unwell man entering the pizza delivery trade at such a late stage in life.

I'll be honest: the fevered brain, caught up as it was in the business of keeping at bay a wave of pain capable of engulfing an entire state, failed to take in much of the day's events. I recall sitting in a village hall and looking at some telly screens, monitoring the shop where we were due to film. I recall meeting some very pleasant people and agreeing that, yes, I was a bit pale and, yes, tired too and that, yes, it's probably because I'd been out to too many late parties in that London. With the filming finally over, I was wafted away from the impromptu set and poured into the back of the car. James was ready up front, hand on the tiller, to guide me back home to my family, my dogs and my painkillers. I looked forward to dozing all the way home.

At about the halfway mark I got the distinct impression that something was not, perhaps, entirely as it should be. Everything was okay with the car, James was chatting merrily and had remembered to replenish his supply of mints kept, for the benefit of his passenger, in the rear ashtray of his Mercedes. The problem lay, it seemed, more close to home. It lay, in fact, in my kidney. It appeared to have grown tired of living in what can't have been very pleasant or roomy quarters, lodged in the gloom and tedium of my intestinal cavity and had, by coincidence, chosen this very evening to make a break for it and head for the wide blue yonder via my spine. I saw stars. I said bad words. I saw vibrant yellow streaks shooting across the night sky, I gripped the headrest in front of me and gritted my teeth and I wondered if perhaps something important had burst or become disconnected inside. As the initial chorus of dazzling agony settled down into a more resolute and steady sort of pain that bore all the hallmarks of being something that would simply dig in and keep going all night, like noisy neighbours with a new stereo, it became clear that, while I was not about to burst inside James's Mercedes like an overripe plum with a grenade inside it, something had gone awry with the stent/kidney situation and had better be addressed sooner rather than later.

James delivered me home and I communicated to Mindy by means of grunts and pointing that something was not as it should be in the region of my recently fettled organ. Mindy obliged by handing me a fistful of painkillers and calling the doctor. The pain built still further and, as if by magic, an ambulance arrived to transport me back to hospital. A doctor removed the stent via the now all too familiar route terminating in that most personal of parts which, in my case, must have boasted heavier traffic in recent days than the Channel Tunnel in mid-August. All of this happened unbeknownst to me, thanks to the merciful slug of morphine that could, from the depth of sleep into which it plunged me, have felled a troupe of insomniac gorillas.

✳

Patched up, polished and delivered home like a mended shoe, I settled back into daily life with, if not my customary degree of physical vim and vigour, at least a merry heart and a happy outlook. The stent was gone, the stone was gone and now, after a short period of recuperation, I could look forward to getting back to normal. The pilot for the – sadly doomed – TV show was looming larger on the horizon and I would soon be busily immersed in excited preparations for the studio day itself. And to my mind anyway, there's absolutely nothing wrong with a brief period of enforced recuperation. I endured a longer period of it a year or so back and, frankly, being obliged by medical practitioners to pop upstairs every afternoon for a couple of hours of shuteye before shuffling back downstairs, catching up on the afternoon telly news, enjoying a light spot of tea and then diving back into the welcoming duvet for another twelve or fourteen hours is not an obligation one should be in a hurry to shrug off. I had been told that a few days at least of gentle activity would be all that was required to bring body and soul back together in perfect harmony and set me back on the busy treadmill with renewed energy and commitment.

And so day one of my short period of recuperation began, gently enough, with breakfast, a flick through the paper, a discussion with Mindy about a friend of a friend's new horse and a brief twinge from my kidney. I tried to resist panicking – though the impulse to tear around the house screaming blue murder and ripping out my hair with fear and despair at what I suspected to be an approaching maelstrom of pain, suffering and indignity did press down upon me strongly. Instead, I rubbed my lower back, as might a gardener having wrestled a particularly recalcitrant sod, pushed my shoulders back and my chest up, puffed out my cheeks and breathed heavily.

'Right, then, I shall spend the day recovering. Not bad, really. A day off, in fact.' I spoke slowly and, breathing out deeply, rubbed my hands together at the breakfast table.

'Are you all right, darling?' Mindy, with a hawk's alertness, had detected something in my manner.

'Nope. I feel like shit and I think there's something up with my kidney.'

'Oh, God.'

'No, no, let's not panic. Just a twinge. I'm going to go and sit in the front room and just ride it through. Look, can't be that bad, I can get up.' And I stood and walked on shaky legs through to the sitting room. Once there, and with the door securely shut behind me, I fell to my knees and reached round to try and somehow squeeze the life out of my kidney and stop it from trying to kill me. It felt angry, as if it should be making a cross noise audible to people around me. And that was just the start, a little something to grab the attention before settling down to the main event. By ten, the old kidney had really got into the groove, stripping off its shirt and flexing its muscles to leave me writhing on the sitting-room carpet like a landed eel at a fisherman's feet. I had considered myself by this stage to be a veteran of kidney pain, having endured three or four stones' passage in the past and, more recently, a veritable street carnival of doctors and nurses trooping through that way waving drills and various devices. This, though, was at an entirely new level.

Having squirmed as much as I could squirm without enduring possibly fatal burns from the sitting-room carpet, I bleated for Mindy to help transport me and my angry kidney upstairs where we might carry on with our heated engagement in a location more conducive, perhaps, to rest and recuperation. It didn't help. In my more lucid moments, those not occupied entirely with moaning and squirming, I tried out some clever techniques for coping with pain. A single red flower of some type – a rose, perhaps, or a geranium, not a daffodil, definitely – stood in a slender green vase on the bedroom windowsill. Using this image as a point on which to fix my wildly veering concentration, I focused on imagining the pain, now growing ever more intense in my lower back, as a small red flower. As the pain intensified, so the flower in my mind's eye grew larger and more beautiful. It was exquisite and it worked – for about ten hours. And then I was sick and could stand no more and Mindy called an ambulance. Annoyingly, morphine didn't seem to touch the pain this time and I continued to squirm about the place making a pretty embarrassing spectacle of myself long after the needle had jabbed and been withdrawn by the paramedics. It seemed inevitable that I would have to be lugged into the ambulance and than transported to the nearest hospital. In between bouts of moaning and being sick, I picked up the medical team's intent to take me to Gloucester hospital.

Keen to take a key role in this whole episode – beyond,

that is, being sick and making a dreadful fuss – I took it upon myself to try and communicate to the ambulance team the nature of my recent condition: the fix administered by the Harley Street doctors, the subsequent rejection by my kidney of the stent and now the sudden onset of this latest bout of pain from the same area. I was anxious, above all, that they should be apprised of the procedures so far carried out on me lest anything the doctors try to do at Gloucester should work to the detriment of or even directly against what had already been done. I tried to communicate all of this in as clear a manner as possible but, in reality, managed only to be sick again and lie on the floor – where I had rolled – with my head in the plastic washing-up bowl fetched up from the kitchen for obvious, though very unpleasant, reasons. In a state of considerable distress, my fevered imagination leaving me convinced, I can only now presume, that I was about to be operated on by some bumbling West Country scarecrow in overalls using shearing clippers as a scalpel, I struggled again to communicate to the paramedics what I felt was information critical to my survival over the next few moments.

'Please,' I tried to say, 'don't administer any further drugs to impair my thought processes or impinge on my level of consciousness because it is absolutely imperative that I apprise the Gloucester medical team of the procedure carried out on me by their counterparts on Harley Street lest they interfere with or render less effective the work hitherto done at, I might add, great personal expense in the private sector.' In the event, I mumbled as best I could and I suspect the ambulance personnel noticed that my head jerked a bit in the bowl and some more sick came out. I was duly ferried on a stretcher to the ambulance and knocked out – to afford, I would guess, some peace and quiet on the short drive to Gloucester as much as for any other reason.

There's something about the tiles they use to clad the ceilings in hospital wards that tunes in directly to the part of your soul that is withering on the vine with the despair and misery and loneliness of it all. The artificial, cheap surface is cratered like the moon, but lacks the romance and mystery of that or any other celestial body. It is a cheap fix for underlying problems of ugliness and unsightliness too expensive to correct in more sincere and meaningful ways. The tiles are a cover-up, an ageing, curling, yellowing architectural sticking plaster. These and other equally bright and uplifting thoughts defined my mood as I lay in a hospital bed in Gloucester, staring at the ceiling and feeling – there's little point in denying it – sorry for myself. In the cold, grey morning light, with the drama of the previous night left behind, it all looked rather sad. I was in a nightie again, and staring up at the all-too-familiar polystyrene tiles.

Then Mindy arrived and the doctor visited to tell us that, yes, I could return home - once more.

Chapter Three

Scared to Death – at 4 MPH

Only once before had I asked someone to take the controls from me; well, when I say 'asked', it was more of a beg, really, a sort of desperate plea from the heart borne out of blind terror and a deep-seated conviction that my co-pilot and I would die if I was left in control for a second longer. I was on my third helicopter-flying lesson a few years back and the tutor decided I was ready to learn how to hover. 'I'll give you the controls,' he told me in that annoyingly calm and authoritative way that helicopter pilots have of telling you even the most mundane of things. I'll bet they ask for a pint of lager and a packet of dry-roasted peanuts in exactly the same tone. And communicate to their wife the most urgent and pressing issues during intimate moments. Anyway, this particular pilot intoned in his most calm and 'I have control of everything and will never, ever panic 'cos I'm a helicopter pilot and much, much cooler than you' manner that he would give me the controls and I could have a go at hovering and he would be standing by to take the controls from me as soon as I asked. Well, that sounded pretty bloody patronising to me and very much like a challenge. I do not, I told him, scare easily, so he had better be ready to take the controls from me if things got a bit hairy. He put the machine in a hover some fifty feet or so above the airfield, I took the stick and we slewed off immediately in a sideways and essentially out-of-control spin. I screamed and begged him to take the stick before we were both killed. I swear the bastard smiled as he did so. And then he said calmly, 'I have control' in that voice. I wanted to punch him but knew that I wouldn't be able to land if I did.

And now, four years later, I faced the same dilemma. Only this time I was not in the sky and the man standing next to me was not a helicopter pilot – or even in control of the machine that was, I was convinced, about to bring about our immediate and spectacular deaths. We were on – and I know this is not going to sound glamorous – the footplate of a traction engine. Yes, I know: hardly a Formula One car, but then I've already driven one of those and made a complete mess of it, as it happens, so this was at least something new.

I had approached the opportunity to 'have a go' on the machine with little more than mild indifference. It had come about in the course of making a programme in my *Engineering Connections* series and so was in the line of duty and therefore came under the huge and growing list of activities that my conscience could class as 'justifiable', should it turn out to be enjoyable, or my patience deem to be 'necessary', if it turned out to be boring. I rather anticipated the latter scenario in this instance. The snorting, hissing beast wheeled itself into view around the side of the workshops run by the engine's owner and I had, upon it parking up next to me, made all the approved oohs and aahs and 'they really don't make them like that any more, do they?' noises at the man driving it. He jumped down from the footplate and clumped about a bit in his big, steel-toe-capped work boots and I surveyed the oily, heavy metal surfaces of the iron horse. It looked as if it weighed about a million tonnes and was about as dynamic as an iceberg. This was not going to be a thrill-of-a-lifetime ride, but we were only half an hour from lunch and I knew where the biggest pasty was in the tuck box, so all would soon be right with my world.

The plan called for me to ride on the footplate of the engine together with the owner/driver bloke and a third man, whom I would be interviewing in the course of filming the programme we were there to make. This third man was a materials scientist, there to talk to me about the remarkable qualities of Teflon, and he had never ridden on a traction engine either. A slender, soft-voiced fellow in his mid-thirties, he looked about as excited as me at the prospect. We were ordered by the director to drive around the car park and along the track surrounding the workshops before returning to our starting point. The trip was only a few hundred yards and would be contained within the safety of the workshop complex. We climbed on and made jokes about there being no seats and the glove box being full of burning coal while the owner hefted a few levers and made manly grunting noises. Finally, he threw a big red lever forward and we set off at three and a half miles an hour on the most terrifying, exciting and dangerous ride of my life. There is no clutch on a traction engine, and it is possessed of an entirely flat torque curve; that is to say, it doesn't set off in the manner traditionally associated with, say, a car, but, rather, releases all of its considerable power in one single and unstoppable dollop of twisting force that drives it from zero to full speed with the immediacy of a falling piano hitting the ground. Okay, so that full speed is only three and a half miles an hour, but the steaming beast then settles into motion at that pace with the inexorable, unstoppable might of tectonic plate movement.

Nothing, it seems, would stop it; not buildings, not roads, not entire towns would hinder its fearsome, plodding progress. Having very, very nearly flown off the back of the footplate with the initial lurch of it setting off and then only avoided rebounding forwards into the lethal, grinding horror of the road wheels in front of me by grabbing hold of a metal bracket protruding from the steam boiler that turned out to be hotter then the sun and burned all of the skin off my palm, I managed to find my feet with a little more security and stare ahead down the top of the boiler through the clouds of scalding steam and the nightmarish whirl of valves, shafts and flywheels. With no tyres between the metal wheels and the road below, the ride was shocking as the full ten tonnes of the machine pressed down through the reverberating rims on to metal ridges designed to help the tractor find grip across rough fields and guaranteed to reduce roads to rippled ruination.

'She narf barggles the fuggin winflop Oi'd farkin' say,' screamed the owner across the racket of the wheels, the engine, the valves and the pistons.

'Er, yes. She does,' I screamed back, deaf, terrified and feeling the blisters grow on my burned palm, 'you mad bastard,' I added, pointlessly, under my breath. The owner/driver stood on the centre of the footplate, hauling on levers, wiping things with his oily rag, spinning the red steering wheel by a handle fixed to its edge and grinning through the steam like the devil himself. I stood to one side, trying to anticipate the lurches of the machine, the better to avoid falling into the blender in front of me. On the other side of the footplate, shadowed by the bulk of the owner/driver, I caught the pale, terrified face of my interviewee. I tried a smile at him, but it came out weak, watery and unconvincing. The noise seemed to rise to a crescendo. The pistons pushed and pulled as the wheels ground the surface below into submission and clouds of angry steam hissed and billowed along the engine's bulging, rivet-pocked flanks. And then the owner was gone. He leapt off the back in pursuit of what I could see on the ground behind was the oil can. It had fallen off the footplate as we rattled across a ridge in the car park. His broad back in blue overalls set off back the way we had come at a gentle lope.

'Where the …' I screamed like a ten-year-old girl and whirled round to look at where we were heading.

'You steer, Rich. Be right back,' the owner bellowed

over his shoulder and stooped to pick up the oil can.

The handle on the steering wheel was hot in my blistered palm. I spun it to the right and stared ahead in complete and terrifying panic. We were heading towards the gates of his compound and beyond them lay the main road. Beyond that lay fields, a small wood and then the town of Ross-on-Wye. We were about to lay waste to the lot, driving through them in an unstoppable riot of steam and noise to leave a ten-foot-wide groove that would head like a rift valley all the way into and through Wales.

'Oh, my God, how the hell do you stop the thing?' I screamed again, my voice now high enough to be heard only by dogs. I spun the steering wheel to the right, feeling no resistance at all while it took up the slack in the chains that connected the steering column to the front wheels far below under the vast, sweating belly of the beast. We would kill people, that was for sure. The survivors would be cross, running from their burning, ruined homes with guns. I pictured scenes somewhere between *Frankenstein's Monster* and *The Wicker Man* unfolding in Welsh fields as we were finally brought to ground when the beast ran out of steam and we were cornered at the end of our newly carved valley. Next to me my interviewee cowered on the footplate, mute with horror. I spun the wheel some more, steering instinctively for the gap in the wire fence ahead, as though imagining that the frail wires might somehow have caused the roaring monster on whose back we rode even a fraction of a second's inconvenience. I drew in a breath and felt the air hot and steam-laden from the engine scalding my lungs as I got ready to scream again for the owner. And then I heard his big boots stepping on to the moving footplate with the surprising grace of a ballet dancer. He smiled and his eyes glittered and I swear I heard him say 'Oi 'ave control' as he hauled in a lever, threw another one forward and the machine ground to a halt ten feet from the main road. The steam hissed around us, gently now as the engine breathed calmly, at last at rest. The interviewee and I looked at each other, aghast and speechless. Friends of the owner had turned up to watch the filming and their children laughed at our still-frightened faces.

Chapter Four

A Dream Come True

There are some things that it would be pretty safe to bet on putting in an appearance on everyone's list of things to do before reaching forty. Many of them are, sadly, a bit too fruity for discussion here. And many of the fruitier 'To Dos' feature more than one participant, I shouldn't wonder. But this is not the forum for discussion of such ideas – there are, I believe, websites where it is possible to hook up with people of a particularly open and broad-minded nature who will happily shoot the breeze on such topics endlessly.

However, there are many more wholesome acts, chal-lenges, ambitions and dreams that are close to universal in the hold they have over those of us drifting closer to the magic age – or perhaps retreating from it and totting up the boxes they omitted to tick en route. These can be said, then, to feature on the Universal List of Things to Do Before You're Forty. And one such thing, I have absolutely no doubt, is to play in a band. The allure of the rock-star lifestyle – the sex appeal, the clothes, the money and, of course, the artistic expression afforded by the opportunity to perform, though mostly just the sex appeal – seems irresistible to us as teenagers; and so, as we approach forty and consider ourselves to be saying goodbye to youthful desires and opportunities, the urge to 'Play in a Band' before it's officially too late becomes close to irresistible. And in recent years I have squared up to that urge, addressed it, given in to it completely and made a Class A, Gold Standard, ocean-going arse of myself in the process. More than once. And it all started with a dream. Well, two dreams, actually.

I'm not sure if anyone really has ever been cursed – or blessed – with the archetypal anxiety dream wherein the key player, the dreamer, passes the midnight hours running naked through a shopping centre. There is, according to the myth, usually a lot of attempting to cover one's most personal portions from the prying eyes of shoppers, police officers and nuns, a lot of running about looking for places to hide and then, when the dreamer awakes, a lot of stuff spoken by experts, analysts and breakfast TV presenters about the dream revealing so many layers of deep-rooted insecurity and anxiety on the part of the dreamer that the analysis of it is likely to prove a more powerful nightmare than the dream itself. This whole naked-in-a-shopping-centre dream might well be something made up by psychologists to play on our neuroses and encourage us to lie on the couch and open our cheque book. But I have no doubt that most of us will, at some point, have been visited by the demons, often in the form of a regularly occurring, recurrent nightmare. If this is you, then I ask that you pour on me your sympathy because I too have been the victim of such a regular visitation with the unique and dreadful extra complication of the dreams subsequently coming true.

For many years, my nightly eight hours of the deep and peaceful were interrupted regularly by one of two recurring dreams. In one scenario I would be presenting a radio programme: something I have done many, many times and generally to reasonably good effect. In the dream version, though, I was hindered in my attempts to keep the listener entertained by my not having the faintest idea of how to operate the broadcast desk by means of which it is possible to play in the records, jingles, news bulletins, weather reports and phone-callers that together make up a radio show.

I would introduce a record and play, instead, the jingle to introduce the news, stumble through an apology, try again to play the record, play the weather jingle instead, open the wrong fader for my microphone and be heard in the far distance apologising to the listener over the microphone kept on the other side of the desk and reserved more ordinarily for interviewees, before finally succeeding in playing in the record successfully, only to open my own microphone fader by accident and be heard, behind the gentle tones of Cat Stevens, saying, 'Shit, I made a right bollocks of that'. It was an uncomfortable moment, even in a dream, and I would generally wake from it in a tortured, sweaty heap with a deep and long-lasting sense of my own hopeless inadequacy and uselessness.

The second dream regularly to stampede its way through my midnight hours and leave a trail of destruction and sweat in its wake would place me in a band, playing on stage to a sizeable gathering of people. This again is a familiar enough situation; I spent large chunks of my formative years playing bass guitar in a range of bands with varying degrees of success but always with a surprising degree of competence and a rewarding display of enjoyment to be observed among those listening to us play. Again, in the dream version, this pleasurable diversion was turned from a platform for confident, assured performance of skills honed and polished over years of practice into an embarrassing and humiliating spectacle in which my confidence, never that high, was brought down lower than a sea slug's undercrackers.

The actual 'gig' featured in my dream would vary, but the sequence of events always ran roughly thus: whether set in a giant arena, a moody blues bar or an international festival stage, I would be slotted into a band of expert musicians with whose repertoire I was entirely unfamiliar. They would play smoothly, cohesively and with emotional involvement and artistic integrity while I mooched about in the background hitting bum notes, tripping over cables, upsetting the beat, losing the chord sequence, playing slap bass solos through the guitar breaks and missing the crescendos.

This dream often left me in an even greater mess on waking than the radio show nightmare and the helplessness, lack of direction and sense of being exposed as a hopeless loon would stay with me sometimes for days.

And, thanks to *Top Gear*, both of these scenarios were dragged from the dark and whirling confines of my dreaming mind and turned into stark, clear reality. In front of millions of people.

The first instance of *Top Gear*'s spooky ability to make dreams come true – in a bad way – came about when we set out to make a film showing how we felt a drive-time radio show should be done. We sort of borrowed a radio station – BBC Southern Counties Radio, thanks for that – and the three of us arrived on site, argued with the programme manager and stampeded off into Studio 1a to host a one-off drive-time radio show our own way.

We were confident that this would make a good film for the telly. Jeremy brought with him some outlandish ideas for encouraging slow drivers on the motorway to get a move on by reading out their car registration numbers on air. James brought with him some fairly left-field ideas for the music playlist that would, he felt, broaden the minds of the listener as he or she switched on their car radio for some company on the commute home. And I brought with me ten years' experience of presenting radio programmes in local radio stations almost identical to the one we had hijacked for the evening. I say 'almost' identical because it would turn out that the 'almost' part was really quite important.

With our assortment of bold ideas, distinctive musical taste and extensive broadcast experience, we settled into the studio with just five minutes to go before we went live to the counties of Sussex and Surrey. I sat at the broadcast desk, from where I would 'drive' the show technically and draw upon my wealth of radio-presenting experience to act as host and kind of tie the whole thing together while Jeremy and James took up positions opposite me at their respective microphones and readied themselves. As they shuffled their papers and laughed at the playlist, I looked at the desk. It was completely different from anything I had ever used before. I may as well have been perched at the control console of a nuclear submarine for all I understood of what any of the array of computer consoles, lights and buttons actually did.

'Er, guys.'

They were still laughing at the playlist and agreeing that we would play our own music and hang the consequences. I tried again, glancing up at the clock to see that we were now only three minutes from going live.

'Guys, I, er, I haven't really sort of, er …' My hands, useless and numb with shock, rested on the smooth board in front of me. I felt a cold sweat spread between my shoulder blades.

'So can you get some decent music on that thing, then?' Jeremy looked up to point a finger at the desk between us.

'Where do they keep the records?' James looked around, expecting to see, I can only imagine, a large cupboard labelled 'Gramophone Records'.

'No, really. Guys, I've never used or even seen a desk like this in my entire life. What the hell does everything do? Where do you switch it on?' I dragged my eye across the high-tech, futuristic panel. I was used to big faders and levers and dials with needles in them that wobbled when you talked or played a record. This was all sleek surfaces, glinting computer screens and discreet buttons set into blank, grey panels. I felt like an astronaut getting settled in on the launch pad for a trip to Mars, only to discover that he had learned how to fly the Mk Two model and this was a Mk Ten.

A technician was summoned and I was given thirty seconds of briefing and then, as the news bulletin ended, I pulled the faders that I had just learned would bring our mics live and launched myself straight into my own recurring nightmare. As Jeremy and James laughed, goofed around and enjoyed themselves, I looked about in wide-eyed panic as a familiar and comfortable world was suddenly made impossible and terrifying. And every single feature from my dream was, over the course of the next two hours, made as real as stone – only a million times more embarrassing. I brought in the sports presenter live when we were expecting the weather; I played the news jingle to introduce the traffic bulletin; I forgot which fader operated which microphone. I may, for all I was aware, have brought down a satellite with one of the three computers banked around me.

This was a *bad* experience. When something with which we are entirely familiar and comfortable is changed just a little, it is often worse than encountering something entirely new for the first time. If I sneaked into your garage and switched the clutch and brake pedals in your car, you would probably find it harder to operate than if you were put in charge of a helicopter for the first time. All of which was, indeed, bad. But not half as gut-wrenchingly, nerve-janglingly, confidence-shred-dingly bad as *Top Gear*'s second bash at making dreams come true.

We had been asked to join in the TV fun and nonsense for the annual Comic Relief Appeal. Comedians, satirists, actors, impresarios and writers from across the world of TV would be lending their talents to create an evening of entertainment and laughter with the aim of encouraging the viewing audience once again to dig deep and help those less fortunate than themselves. Although, right now, as we sat in the *Top Gear* production office and wracked our respective brains for anything we could possibly do to add to the forthcoming feast of charitable comedy efforts, it was difficult to think of anyone in the world actually less fortunate than us.

I shan't list the ideas with which we had, by now, toyed, but it had been long, exhaustive and almost entirely use-less. Andy Wilman, the boss, had volunteered us for this duty out of the finest of motives and we had agreed to it, out of interest, largely, but now, as we slumped in chairs around the office and contemplated what sort of contri-bution we could possibly make to an evening of comedy featuring the funniest men and women in the country, we realised we might all have been a little rash.

It is evidence enough of the extent of our explorations into the subject and of the list of ideas rejected that we reached a point at which someone raised the subject of the recent termination of *Top of The Pops* and suggested we had a go at bringing it back. And it is further evidence of our exhaustion and panic that we agreed unanimously that this was the best idea so far and began immediately to investigate just how to go about doing this.

The idea sort of snowballed, as they often do. Well, some ideas snowball: the large, sticky ones mostly. Smaller, classy ideas don't snowball; they stay pure and unsullied and are executed by efficient, focused professionals with a strong sense of staying true to the perceptive force and conceptual clarity of the original idea itself. This one snowballed like a bugger, though, picking up extra bits, additional ideas and people just like a real snowball rolling down a hill picks up gravel, bits of stick and dog turds before smashing into a wall at the bottom and being reduced to a pile of slush and compost.

We would, as the idea now ran, host the first – and almost certainly only – *Top Gear of The Pops*. Bands were invited and, amazingly, all agreed to come on and do a turn for the show: McFly, Travis, Supergrass and Lethal Bizzle. All signed up out of generosity and a sense of mucking in and helping out in the name of charity. The bands would play, our crew would film them, we three presenters would present it and the *Top Gear* studio audience would, well, they would do the audiencing.

It became a concept: the programme would be a sort of hybrid created by the fusing of two long-running and significant BBC brands. But we couldn't stop meddling; the snowball wouldn't stop rolling. And, soon enough, we rolled over a truly momentous turd and it stuck to the side of our snowball. Somebody, certainly not me, suggested that we three, rather than limiting ourselves purely to the role of presenters, doing the boring talkie bits between the bands, take the concept a step further and become one of the bands as well. And while I have gone to great pains to establish that this suggestion definitely was not made by me, I am ashamed to confess that when our snowball rolled over to reveal this especially claggy and unpleasant addition stuck to its bulging flank, I failed to do the sensible, adult thing and threaten to hold my breath until it went away, but, rather, I joined in with the clamouring and shouting and agreed that, yes, it was a blinder and we must do it. Of course we must.

James is an accomplished piano player, having studied music at Lancaster University. I have played bass for twenty-five years in a range of bands to a semi-professional degree and Jeremy was a veteran of three drum lessons. Perfect. How could we fail? Well, pretty easily, in fact, given that we didn't have a singer. Andy Wilman had, it turned out, operated as a singer in a few bands over the years and would be more than capable of yelping along to whatever song we decided to play – and that was a discussion to look forward to if ever there was one – but didn't have, he felt, the necessary star qualities to act as a draw for our performance. What we needed, he told us, was an actual, famous singer from an actual, famous band.

The thing to do, then, was to ask the singer from a current pop band if he wouldn't mind stepping in and threatening his dignity, career and livelihood by moonlighting with our soon-to-be-formed supergroup. We had not yet agreed on a song to perform – though we had already endured a lengthy and, if I am honest, fiery discussion or two over a beer on this matter. But we felt pretty confident that whatever number we did finally settle upon – and there could yet be blood shed over the matter – it would be something more suited to the impressive vocal style and range of Justin Hawkins of The Darkness. And, bloody hell if he didn't then agree to do it.

It seemed that we were already an unstoppable musical force. There must have been musical gods looking down and bestowing on us humble minstrels their favour. We were blessed with a singer of skill, charm and international reputation. We already had a platform for our first performance that would put us in front of millions of people. And it was all in the name of charity. This, then, was the real-life version of the Blues Brothers, only bigger and better. All we needed was a song.

I can't go into too much detail concerning the discussions we had to find the song we would perform. This is not for legal reasons and it's certainly not out of sensitivity for the feelings of the key personnel involved. My brain has simply edited out large chunks of what went on. It is, in short, too awful to recall. Try it for yourself. Get hold of any three mates who have never played together in a band, put them in a bar and ask them to agree on a song to perform in front of a few million television viewers. It will be funny. But stand a long way back when they start talking. I would advise getting things going and then leaving them to it while you take a flight that requires, on landing, the adjustment of your watch by at least eight hours.

The final suggestion came, as if it need be stated here,

from Mr J. Clarkson of Chipping Norton. We had, in the early stages of our discussion, agreed that we were somewhat limited in our choice of numbers by the experience of the rhythm section of our fledgling ensemble. That is to say, Jeremy had only recently taken up the drums and couldn't really play anything that required much beyond a fairly basic 'boom, crash, boom, boom crash'. But he was man enough to confess quite freely to this shortcoming and we determined to pinpoint a mutually agreeable track that matched our mixed range of preferences, experience, aspirations and ability.

After several sessions of what might at best be euphemistically termed 'heated debate', it still seemed that the elusive track might never be found. But we continued to exercise our brains in the pursuit of 'The Song' at every opportunity. There are, in some debating chambers, reams of conventions to be upheld and adhered to concerning manner of expression and address, order and priority of speaking and even clothing. None of these applied as we gathered around a large table in the private conference room of a cheap hotel in the Midlands. We were staying there that night to shoot a completely different film for *Top Gear* the following day, but, as we were all together, the conversation was dominated entirely by the ongoing and ever-more pressing search for a song.

The problem of unanimously agreeing on a song was exacerbated, perhaps, by the fact that a number of us around the debating table were bearing down on or slowly retreating from the age of forty. At about this stage of life, music assumes a new significance. The business of favouring one band over another is tied up with a great deal of stuff about fashion, upbringing, teenage aspirations, regional ties, self-image and social positioning – precisely the sort of concerns that keep a chap in his late thirties awake at night. Any discussion centring on musical preferences, therefore, drags up some pretty sensitive issues for a bloke in the later stages of his approach to forty.

What makes it worse is the fact that those already past the landmark age are often intent on establishing that theirs is the better position than the one occupied by the younger conversationalists. And this is done in a way not entirely as mature and sophisticated as might be expected from the older members of any group.

'What, you don't remember all the lyrics of "Pinball Wizard"? Duh, what a loser!'

'Yeah, how can you not remember everything The Who ever did? God, *what* a loser. They were great. We all loved them. I remember we used to …' and then there'll be a lot of talk about outlandish outfits, outrageous and mostly fictitious parties and concerts and a meaningful examination of lyrics recalled from the back of record sleeves read in dingy student flats centuries ago.

All of which could have been shut down by the simple expedient of pointing out that one's inability to remember the band under discussion stems not from some social, intellectual or spiritual shortcoming, but is an inevitable function of one's comparable youth when in the company of men clearly the best part of a generation older. In the event, what I did instead was pretend I could remember the band under discussion and then try and bluff my way through it when the conversation boiled down to specific concerts, lyrics and album covers. Needless to say, it was quite a stressful evening and I freely admit here that I understood not more than 5 per cent of what was said. And we finished that and several more evenings without coming to a conclusion.

And then, one morning, Jeremy arrived in the office breathless with excitement. He had, he declared, got it: the mystery was solved, the question answered, the quest over. We gathered around him like so many musical seagulls with their beaks open, and we begged him to gift us with the knowledge he had brought back.

'"Red Light Spells Danger." Billy Ocean.'

There was a bit of a pause during which we each tried on a facial expression that we thought might best fit the moment. I veered from acknowledgement to light scepticism before eventually settling on puzzlement.

'Never heard of it.'

'It's perfect.' And he sang a few bars while miming the act of drumming.

I still couldn't recall it, and neither could most of the rest of the team. But we agreed that it sounded, at least from Jeremy's impromptu rendition, achievable. A rehearsal hall was duly booked and, on the agreed date, a rehearsal undertaken. Jeremy could indeed manage to keep the beat to this particular track, James successfully bashed out a few relevant chords on the keyboard and I pulled a string or two at what seemed like the appropriate moments. Without a singer to rehearse the song itself it was hard to polish the band's performance to perfection, but we felt sure that, by surfing on the wave of our combined talent, we could make it work on the night. And, anyway, there is such a thing as being over-rehearsed and we certainly didn't want to fall into that trap.

All of which explains how, on 11 March 2007, I had the rare and unforgettable experience of seeing a long-term recurring dream made real. It felt very much as I imagine it used to feel for real bands playing on the real *Top of The Pops*: the studio moodily lit, the various bands busying themselves on several stages, setting up drum kits and amplifiers and sound-checking with the technicians. I stood on our stage, a large one occupying the back wall of our strangely transformed studio, and looked around me. To my left, McFly ran through a last-minute rehearsal of their number. Young, shiny-haired and bright, they exuded confidence and ability. Backstage, I knew that Travis were relaxing before their performance. To my immediate right, Jeremy's arse could be seen sticking out from behind his drum kit as he searched underneath for a dropped drumstick. James was playing Bach on his keyboard. Justin Hawkins stood at the front and I couldn't see but could guess his expression. I imagine one or other of his eyebrows was crawling up his forehead at a brisk pace as the realisation of the degree of talent absent from his new band settled in and made itself comfortable.

What seemed like seconds later, we were back on the same stage, only this time, gathered around us, was the studio audience. Punctuating the crowd were the glinting lenses of the same cameras that pointed at us week after week in the course of recording our *Top Gear* show. Only this time they were waiting for us to perform as a band. An air of expectant hush descended. The floor manager, his grin sticking out from either side of his headphones with the pleasure of his new role, waved his arms and shouted that all cameras were rolling and we were ready to record. And, like a ski-jumper making his first-ever descent of the ramp, we were off. And God it was bad.

We wobbled through the first few bars like a fawn taking its first steps. It's a gentle starter, 'Red Light Spells Danger'; the drums, bass and keyboard run through the chord sequence at a sensible, controlled pace and the singer joins in with an early rendition of the chorus at a kind of three-quarter performance level. It's a comfortable, easy sort of a thing for a band's first outing. We plodded on doggedly, dropping a note here and there, but making a decent enough hash of it. Justin was great; long hair draped across the mic as he swung himself into a role so familiar to him, though made somewhat less so by the presence behind him of three grinning loons from a TV car show rather than what you might call an actual band. The audience were still with us, though, buzzing with an initial charge of excitement at realising we really were going to give it a shot. This felt good.

With a previous band I had once played a large club somewhere in Yorkshire, only to get about as far into the first song as we had got today and have the landlord pull the plug and eject us. He was under the impression he had booked a semi-acoustic jazz outfit to tickle his punters' ears rather than a very much electrified funk–jazz–blues combo full of beer and boyish enthusiasm coming charging into the room at a million miles an hour with 'Hoochie Coochie Man'. Nobody pulled the plug today, though, and we moved on through the one song that made up our repertoire.

The bridge was arriving, the point at which the music swells with emotion and pace and drive and really picks up. It's a great moment in any song and in this particular one, whatever your own tastes might be, there is no doubting that it's a good example of that moment when a song simply takes hold of you and makes you feel good. And it was down to us to bring about that swell. I readied myself to drive the bass line harder, make the individual notes punchier and crisper. James would beef up the keyboards, throwing in swooshy strings and a fatter sound to fill the whole thing in a bit. Justin would suddenly elevate his performance, switching from three-quarters to full-on rock star stuff; it was this that would give the song the sense of release as it burst forth. But the real driver at this point, the force behind the charge, would be the drums. With a roll round the kit, the drummer signals a change of mood and tempo and pushes the thing harder. There is no actual speeding up, but it feels that way as it all becomes brighter, harder and more confident.

The bridge was ticking nearer and nearer to us by the beat. I looked around to see the studio audience actually starting to sway and bob their heads; if we got the next moment right they would be swept away completely. And that moment was fast approaching. This was it. This would require every ounce of coordination, control and cooperation we could muster. We played on, the last few beats now to the bridge.

The start of the swell would not be signalled by Justin; the song calls for the singer to give away nothing of what is about to come. The start of it is signalled by a single syncopated snare beat; it's like the start of a dam bursting. I waited for the single, bright snap of the snare, like a cork leaving a champagne bottle. It came; Jeremy hit one and then another crystal-clear rap on the snare and a single tom-tom and we were off. Justin's voice took the swelling upsurge of the keyboards with it and I went with them, pushing the notes out of the bass now, damping as hard as I was playing with left and right hands to keep the notes punchy and bright, careful to rein in the charge and not let it get away, to contain and control the energy and present it to the audience as a measured, crafted thing. James pushed a string section into the mix with his right hand, thickening the sound and Justin revelled in it at the front, moving faster now, bouncing on his feet and gripping the mic close to his face. I looked across at Jeremy, keen to establish that almost telepathic link between bassist and drummer that can define a band's sound and give it a rock-solid platform from which to leap into the stormy waters of extemporisation and improvisation or bring the whole thing home with metronomic precision and regularity.

Then he dropped a drumstick.

I saw his head drop down to the skin of the snare as his right arm felt under the bass drum for the stick and I felt the wheels come off our performance. He found it, looked up and grinned at me over the drum and swung back into action, half a beat behind. I missed a note, tripped over the next one and slipped a gear entirely with the pace, leaving Jeremy nothing to climb back into. In short, it all turned to shite until the audience were listening to something roughly a notch and a half below what you might expect from a poorly rehearsed school band at a half-term concert. *Top Gear* had gifted me with another dream come true.

Chapter Five

Flat Out on the Salt Flats

I make no secret of the fact that I love American muscle cars of the 1960s. This is a significant confession and makes me deeply unpopular with pretty much everyone in the world. Car nuts hate American muscle cars of the 1960s because they're poorly made and inefficient. Car haters hate them because they are the pinnacles of auto-motive excess, dripping oil and testosterone. The only people who like them, in fact, are the ranks of the spe-cialist muscle car clubs. And they are, well, I don't wish to be rude, but they are generally pretty awful.

The thing is, though, that there are some likes and dis-likes that a chap can't explain or justify, but that are more deeply rooted in his soul than the desire to breathe or reproduce. I cannot bear, for instance, to see packets of dried pasta in the kitchen. It's not that I don't enjoy a plate of pasta or that I connect the sight of the stuff in its dried state with some ghastly childhood linguini inci-dent. The sight just depresses me and it doesn't, quite frankly, bear analysis. And so it is with my love for muscle cars. To some they are symbols of all that is bad about American excess, with their acres of poorly executed chrome trim and their huge, inefficient engines gargling fuel at a rate prodigious enough that they run the risk not only of damaging the natural habitat of the world's most rare and precious creatures but of actually ingesting penguins into their massive cylinders and turning them – inefficiently – into a huge amount of noise and a small amount of forward motion. They are showy, brassy, crass, poorly engineered, overrated and, if you are of a particular mindset, namely mine, irresistibly gorgeous. I tell you these facts about muscle cars and my love of them the better to prepare your imagination for trying to picture my response when it was mooted in the *Top Gear* office that the three of us, me, James and Jeremy, travel to America, pick up the three latest and greatest incarnations of the all-American muscle car and drive them across a couple of states, ending up with high-speed runs at the legendary Bonneville Salt Flats where people have been racing muscle cars from the precise second that muscle cars arrived on this earth. To say, then, that I was enthusiastic doesn't quite cover it. A slightly damp, sweaty sensation crept across my chest and fought for attention with my scalp, which appeared to be trying to screw itself up and leap into the air when details of this plan were first voiced.

'Oh, I see. So we take the new Dodge Challenger, a V8 Cadillac CTS-V and a Corvette ZR1 across Nevada, back to the home of drag racing and run them at full speed on the Salt Flats. Nice.' I tried to keep the tremor out of my voice as I asked the researcher who had broken the news of this latest wheeze to me for clarification.

'Yup. And seeing as you're the big muscle car fan, the idea is that you get the Challenger.' The researcher smiled benignly and retreated back into his pile of paperwork like a poorly turned-out fairy godmother putting her wand away and popping back to wherever she came from, having granted a recovering alcoholic the keys to the wine cellar and a note from his doctor. This was one of those moments – and there have been a few over the past seven years – when a spot of pinching of self was called for as I tried to digest the fact that another childhood dream appeared to have leapt up off the page and tapped me on the shoulder. The Bonneville Salt Flats: huge expanses of glaring whiteness spreading starkly across the desert floor of Utah like spilt milk on the moon had called to me from the pages of, it seemed, every well-thumbed childhood encyclopaedia-of-exciting-stuff-that-boys-need-to-know-about that I had opened by torchlight under the covers. They have been the site of hundreds of world records set and broken since 1914 (300mph – Malcolm Campbell in 1935, 400mph, 500mph and 630.39mph, the last record, in 1970). And the Dodge Challenger, made famous in the 1970s film *Vanishing Point* starring Barry Newman – is about the most famous muscle car of all. Ugly, overpowered, under-engineered and, frankly, lethal, it is a name so charged with all that makes up a muscle car that I could hardly say it aloud without it coming out all breathy and hot. And I would be taking the latest incarnation of this legend to the Bonneville Salt Flats. As my job.

'Yeah, okay. Sounds good.' I tried to appear nonchalant and cool but it may have come out a bit squeaky.

Of course many people have died racing cars on the Salt Flats over the past century. And *Vanishing Point* ends with Barry Newman stuffing his Challenger into a digger bucket and being killed in a huge fireball. These thoughts, though, were not among those now churning hotly around my head as I wandered off to the coffee machine and reached for my phone to call my wife, Mindy.

※

Some weeks and a very great deal of daydreaming later …

In San Francisco we filmed the bit where we all three arrive with our cars and discuss what we have, how we got it and why it's better than anything the others have. I tried to concentrate on the work at hand but my eyes saw only visions of arrow-straight roads across the desert heading towards a distant but growing patch of what appeared to be ice on the desert floor but would turn out to be the Salt Flats, and my ears heard nothing but the monotonous, gritty drone of the big V8 settling in for the long charge to glory.

And the Salt Flats really did appear on the distant horizon like a patch of spilt milk, spreading and growing until my whole field of vision was filled by the dazzling white expanse. The Challenger's big V8 hauled the horizon in with a dreadful, unstoppable monotony, roaring its defiance to the broad blue skies. Comfortable now in the car's workaday, blue-collar interior after hundreds of miles spent staring ahead and holding the wheel with an arm propped on the door, I smiled slowly and dreamed of speed as the last miles ticked by.

Something else of which I am inordinately fond, and of which said fondness I am not especially proud, are the paintings of Jack Vettriano. They're not exactly dripping with serious, artistic intent and to some, art professors and the like, are as cheesy and openly sentimental as the famed Athena posters of the 1980s. Many of which, coincidentally, featured the strikingly lit, wilfully posed paintings of this Scottish canvas dauber. And to compound this sin in the eyes of certain factions of the artistic establishment, I am especially fond of the series of paintings he produced depicting scenes of Malcolm Campbell's 1935 assault on the land speed record in his famous Bluebird.

Upon stepping out of my Challenger and setting foot on to the starched surface of the Bonneville Salt Flats for the first time, I realised immediately that the heightened, almost caricatured lighting of Vettriano's paintings in no way overemphasises the reality. It may simply be a function of the sunlight bouncing up off the salt that acts as a giant reflector to throw thick slabs of white light on to angles and planes not normally highlighted that creates an unworldly scene of electric vitality. But it is a sight possessed of an unworldly, magical quality.

I stood by the still-warm flanks of the Challenger, resting a hand on the hot bonnet, and surveyed the milling ranks of drivers and support crews variously tending to their steeds, discussing tactics or perhaps commiserating private failures. Failures dictated by the timing lights away down the parched strips of salt where their run had ended with numbers only fractions of a second beyond what they had hoped for, but a world away from those they were determined to return to boast about to their workmates in their home state.

The place works to a unique rhythm; a pace born of the process of collecting thoughts and dreams and preparing the machine for the wait at the start line, the agonising seconds before the signal is sent at the speed of light to hit the throttle and test the work of the team and their dreams in a headlong, crazy charge across the white plain before bursting across the finish line. Then they must cruise round to the tiny shed with peeling blue paint on its door, out of which steps the timing official wearing a straw hat. The drivers know before they look at the white paper slip handed them by the official if the news is good or bad. They will each have shared, on previous runs, their desired aim with him and his face, bearing a grin or a frown, will have told them all they need to know before they strain their sweat-stung eyes to read the legend on the faded printout passed through the open window.

It is a routine practised through the decades and handed down from dreamer to dreamer with all the sombre attention to detail and magic of any human ritual. Metal workers, welders, construction workers, accountants, dot.com millionaires, film stars and playboys have gathered on this salt, stripped of their status and everyday rank by the overalls, sun hats and upsurging sunlight from the salt on which they hope to make their longed-for dash for glory. Then my time came.

I waited on the line. My car growled and shook. I felt it strain and coil itself and I felt the line itself, waiting for me. Asking the same question of me as it had asked of countless thousands before. Ahead, through the suddenly crystal-clear windscreen, lay the sparkling Salt Flats that had hosted glories, shattered dreams and caused death. And I was, I don't mind admitting now, scared. I saw my own crash unfolding again before me, I saw the tyre burst, I felt the car shift and roll to the right. I felt the cold steel of the parachute-release lever in my right hand and I knew again the sudden disappointment of its failure to stop me rolling. And dying. And I died again in my mind and knew again the moment of certainty when all that can come is the end.

I knew that today would not bring such a thing again, that I was at the wheel of a standard car that had undergone tens of thousands of hours of careful testing ready to be sold to a million customers with lives important and precious, and that the builders and designers had known this and made sure that their creation would be as safe as it could be. But the magic of the Flats had infiltrated me, had run through my innermost being and I sat now on the verge of something huge and terrifying but made clear by the starkness of the parched salt itself.

The lights changed. I hit the throttle, not stabbing it wildly but pushing it forwards, feeling the wheels tear into the salt, find their grip and surge the car forward.

Driving fast on salt is somewhere between driving on ice and sand. I felt the wheels drift and claw their way through the top layer of powder, pushing aside shallow, fat tracks in the salt. The engine bellowed and roared, happy to be freed from the line and we charged for the end of the strip. I passed the lights. I let the car slow at its own pace, leaving the brakes alone and drove slowly around the marked path towards the hut with the blue door and controlled my breathing as I approached. I don't remember the time I set. I don't remember what time I was hoping for. None of this went into the film we made. It was private, and I feel better for sharing it.

Chapter Six

Ticking the Box

It's funny how these things crop up. This was a big one –
and not just on my list. I'm sure that acting in a film
appears on the list of 'things to do before the age of forty'
for ninety-eight per cent of males. And the opportunity to
tick that very box had just landed square in my lap. I
braced up and prepared myself once more to deliver a
contained and dignified acceptance of an offer that, quite
frankly, had me streaming with sweat and excitement. I
played it cool.

'Er, yes. That'd be great, thanks. I'd love to.' I held the
phone away from my ear briefly and bent double,
punching the air at midriff height and mouthing the
word 'Yesssss' in tones hopefully too hushed for the BBC
executive on the other end of the line to hear.

The cause of my barely contained outburst was a request
from Elaine Paterson to take part in a special, one-off short
film with the team from the excellent *Ashes to Ashes* TV
drama for the annual BBC Children in Need Appeal. What
it amounted to, then, was a request for me to rally round

and join in with the noble, charitable efforts of people from across the country on behalf of those less fortunate than themselves. The exact nature of that rallying would, in my case, not be anything that could reasonably be considered even remotely onerous. It would represent the realisation of a lifelong ambition: I would be taking to the silver screen in a film as an actor. Specifically, I would be starring opposite Phil Glenister, who plays the legendary Gene Hunt, and the rest of the actors in what remains one of my absolute favourite TV dramas, the cops/coma/time travel comedy series, *Ashes to Ashes*. It would be, I should stress, a short film. A very short film, in fact, probably a couple of minutes at best. And my role, from what Elaine had outlined to me over the phone, would be to recreate what might perhaps be euphemistically termed my 'role' on *Top Gear* every week. That is to say, I would be playing myself. I was at least pretty sure that I could carry this one off, probably better than anyone else.

'Yes, smashing – really, I'd *love* to – not a problem. Not at all. Thanks for asking me.' We discussed the project, Elaine reassuring me that it would be a valuable and useful contribution to the night of entertainment she and the team had planned for Children in Need. And would play its part in encouraging the ever generous British people to dig deep and lend their financial and spiritual support to needy children in the most dire circumstances at home and around the globe.

'And, er, do I have to wear anything in particular?'

'I think we can leave that to the production team really, Richard.'

On hallowed ground –
the Bonneville Salt Flats Raceway,
Utah.

Following the tracks of legends. I would be lying if I said I wasn't a tiny bit scared.

Muscle cars, salt flats, mountains – and filming. I am as happy as a pig in salt.

Another box ticked – a world tour before the age of 40. With Jeremy and Steve Pizzati in Sydney

A helicopter pre-crash. It looked much the same post-crash but the seagull didn't.

'Yes, yes. Of course. Who cares what I wear anyway? Hah, just some bloke off *Top Gear* joining in with the pros for an afternoon, hey? So is there a wardrobe then or shall I just wear something from *Top Gear*?'

I was running on rather, not giving Elaine a chance to interject and answer the questions now stacking around my head like aircraft waiting their turn to get into Heathrow on a busy morning.

'I'll just wear jeans and a shirt. Yes. Just like normal. I'll not panic about it, don't you worry. So when do they send me a script?'

Arrangements were made and, in due course, a script dropped on to the mat. I stood by the front door and looked at it, seeing in my mind's eye a shaft of light slanting down through the windows and playing upon it as a choir sang uplifting chords to signify that this was the start of something of immense importance. I've always wanted to be an actor and my imagination had, perhaps, got a little carried away with the significance of my bit-part cameo in a short TV sketch for charity. Nevertheless, I scooped up the envelope, ripped it open and tried to read the contents in the way I felt a real actor might read a script. That is, I tried to see past the words and really dig deep into the narrative to find the truth in my role and the best way of bringing about a connection with the audience. It was tricky really, because as far as I could see, I had to pretend to be looking at an old Audi which Phil Glenister, as Gene Hunt, would pretend was his and he and the gang from the TV show would arrive and pretend to be cross. I would pretend to ask if I could have a go. Philip Glenister/Gene Hunt, would say yes. I would pretend to have a go and then drive off with the sexy policewoman played by Keeley Hawes who would pretend to be frightfully enamoured of the idea of going off in the car with me rather than spending her time with her cronies from the station. This last bit would, of course, require some masterful Method acting from Keeley who, while able to carry off the sexy bit with aplomb and a natural ease, might struggle a bit to pretend that she was remotely keen to slip into a rusty saloon car with a short bloke from a car show she had probably never seen. I read and reread the script until the paper itself wore the crumpled and worn-thin appearance of a treasure map or a court summons.

The day arrived, as they do. I had stayed in London the previous night – it seemed the thing to do before my acting debut – and the morning found me slumped in a tangled heap of bedclothes and nerves. I roused myself from shallow, tortured sleep in the stifling heat of my flat and padded around the place in socks and a dressing gown, running through my lines and preparing myself to get into character. I would have preferred to switch on an elaborate Italian coffee machine and run through my lines to the music of its operatic gurglings as it prepared a brew of such strength and ferocity that only a truly sophisticated actor such as myself could deal with it, perhaps after a particularly louche and actorly night on the tiles with some actor chums in my actors' club. As it was, I don't actually have a coffee machine, so I spooned Nescafé into a mug with a Union Jack on it and sat at the table with the now barely legible script spread before me on the table.

There really wasn't much to it. The scene – and there really was only one scene involved in the project – would open with what I presumed would be a long, lingering shot of me, as me, running a hand along the red flanks of Gene Hunt's Audi Quattro. I ran a hand along the table top, trying to force through the tendons and veins a visible sense of longing and admiration for an imaginary car until I was sure that the camera would pick it up when the time came. There would then be, as far as I had been able to deduce from the, frankly, rather thin script, a long and doubtless lingering shot of my hollow-cheeked, actorly face as I took in the details of what I was now preparing myself to think of as a car possessed of such grace and beauty that it must tear at the heartstrings like an axe at a violin. I practised what I felt was a look that sort of summed this up. Phil Glenister, as Gene Hunt, would then shout, off camera. I read the line: 'Oi', he would shout. And I prepared myself for this, readying my head to snap up sharply in surprise at this entirely unexpected interjection into my automotive reverie. I practised raising an eyebrow to accentuate the effect. Thinking that I had best be sure of the effect of this move as it could be a crucial piece of artifice in conveying the shock of this untimely outburst to a man who really had been lost in thought, I dashed through to the bathroom to check it out in the mirror. It looked good; after some practice I decided that my left eyebrow best expressed the desired combination of surprise and fear mixed with a twist of indignation at being interrupted, though I readied myself to deploy the right one if camera angles or lighting directors demanded it.

I returned to the table and smoothed the crumpled script with a steady hand. And now, having heard Gene Hunt's exclamation and raised an eyebrow, it was time for my first line. With left eyebrow raised to maximum angle and head twisted up and to the left, I breathed and then went for it; speaking my line into the hushed silence of my flat as sincerely as though to a crammed and expectant auditorium at the Royal Shakespeare in Stratford.

'Sorry?'

It sounded wrong. I took the question out of it and tried it again.

'Sorry.' My voice had sunk too far at the end; it brought a sense of finality that would, I knew, signal closure of the piece rather than the beginning of a relationship between Phil Glenister, as Gene Hunt, and me, as me. I tried it again with a lighter inflection and quite deliberately, and with infinite care, allowed a trace of nervousness to tinge the second syllable and colour the whole line with a sense of fragility and vulnerability that would, I felt sure, resonate within the hearts and souls of the audience.

'Sorry.' It was perfect. I ran through it a dozen or so times more, honing it, polishing it and making it shine until I knew it was fit to show to anyone. I read the next line. Phil Glenister, as Gene Hunt, would then enquire of me, as me, as to the nature of my present physical engagement with his precious car.

'Get away from that motor,' he would say, 'and put your

hands in the air.' In my actor's mind, I actually heard him say the line: I heard the steely-edged, Mancunian twang of Gene Hunt's nasal voice. And I replied, naturally, easily and believably, lost in the part now. This was Method, I was sure.

'Thing is,' and then there were some dots on the script which I interpreted, correctly, as indicating to the actor – me, as me – that they might, for dramatic effect, insert a pause at this point. I did insert a pause: quite a big one. During which pause I made my eyes reflect the desire I felt for the car, the need I had been unable to restrain in me to touch it and, perhaps, the memories of a childhood spent without access to such luxuries bubbling up now to drive this normally shy and diffident character to such an act of wanton and confident physicality with another man's car. I went on with my lines.

'… it's such a magnificent car. I was wondering if …' and there were some more dots. I took a break in this pause to make a cup of tea and calm myself. I have heard actors speak of the draining effect of practising their art and I understood that effect now. My soul felt both diminished by the effort and strangely fulfilled by the act of creation.

After an hour or so, I had progressed through the entire script. The piece would run, I figured from my own solo run-through of it from beginning to end, to about three minutes and twenty-five seconds. It would be, I felt sure, intense. People watching would be engaged by it and moved to donate large sums of money to the charity. If, as a by-product of this charitable act, I were to be picked up by an agency and begin a new career as a film actor, well, that would in no way detract from the primary purpose of the piece in generating those charitable donations from the viewers, compelled by the enjoyment they had gained from our acting, to give money for the benefit of others. I was ready. I had combed through my lines, groomed them until they shone with health and vigour and life and I was ready now to show them to the world. And so I left for the set.

A film set is, it would seem, much like the television sets with which I am more than familiar. The usual collection of vans and hire cars disgorge a series of people carrying boxes and crates out of which emerge cameras, lenses, sound booms and rolls of the ubiquitous gaffer tape. The prime difference, perhaps, was the presence on site of a catering wagon. From the open hatch of a small caravan one could obtain tea, coffee, bacon sandwiches and biscuits at any time of one's own choosing and in any quantity. I was, sadly, too nervous to take advantage of the bacon sandwiches but made free with the tea while I waited for my fellow actors to arrive. I was quite early.

One by one they did arrive, though. And I felt the energy levels rise on set with the arrival of each member of the ensemble. At least, I'm pretty sure I did It seemed the sort of thing a real actor would think, so I tried to think it. Dean Andrews and Marshall Lancaster gathered around the catering van to share tea and stories. We spoke about *Top Gear* and about *Ashes to Ashes*. I looked into their faces and tried to imagine standing in front of them and going through the lines I had rehearsed. Eventually, I felt another burst of energy, which could only mean one thing; well, it could always have been indigestion, of course, but more likely it meant that, with the rest of the team already on site, Phil Glenister was here. A rangy, energetic man brimming with contained energy, he strode through the group, suppressing his personality and keeping himself small and quiet – conserving energy, perhaps, for the acting to come.

'Y'all right then, cocker?' He clapped me on the back. I went to speak but only just stopped myself from blurting out 'Sorry' and then waiting for Phil Glenister, as Gene Hunt, to say, 'Get away from that motor and put your hands in the air.'

''Ow's Jezza then? Your show's good these days, innit? This lot always watch it.' He tilted his head to take in the rest of the group, who variously busied themselves stirring coffee, smiling or lighting fags.

Make-up was applied, lights were set, cameras readied and, in a fine drizzle, we gathered around the car, ready to begin our scene. I breathed slowly and tilted my head back to look up past the high brick walls that made up the warehouse complex surrounding the rough-floored parking lot where we were working. The red Audi Quattro was immediately to my left. I put out a hand to brush its flanks, feeling the thick bubbles of rainwater burst luxuriantly against its polished surface and then snatching my hand away quickly before anyone saw that I had left a trail through the raindrops that would reveal to the camera that this was clearly not the first time my hand had trailed this way. No matter: more rain would fall and replace it.

The director, a smart young bloke with very short hair and fashionably nondescript clothes, brought us all to order. I heard his words almost as though my ears were full of water. I was in something like a trance as I readied my entire being for my first steps into the world of acting.

'And … Action.' The camera assistant had used an actual clapperboard with numbers on it in front of the camera and everything immediately before the director called for Action in clipped, confident tones. And I began. I walked alongside the car, feeling the lens as it followed my hand's adoring path along the car's bonnet. I breathed an audible sigh, the better to accentuate, I thought, the feelings that I, as me, had for this machine that had been so far beyond my reach as a youth and which now lay, materially and viscerally, beneath my hand. Without looking up, I was aware of Phil Glenister, as Gene Hunt, and his crew moving towards me. They would intercept me as I reached the front of the bonnet. I resisted looking up and stared fixedly at my hand. I saw the polished shoes of Phil Genister as Gene Hunt step forward, almost touching the car's front bumper. I breathed: one breath: a beginning. And I spoke.

'Sorry.' And I snapped my head up, left eyebrow deployed to the absolute maximum. Silence greeted me. And then …

'I'm supposed to say "Oi" first, mate.'

I had pre-empted the interjection of Phil Glenister as

Gene Hunt. This was the equivalent of a child actor in a school play shouting 'come in' two seconds before the door has been knocked on. They must have seen the horror in my eyes; they must have seen the despair that followed. They must have seen these things because they waited a discreet second or two before laughing. Once they'd given in, though, they really went for it. I joined in. There was nothing else to do and if I was honest, to me – really as me and not acting as me – it was a bubble burst as surely as the bubbles of rainwater burst under my hand on the red flanks of the Audi Quattro belonging to Phil Glenister as Gene Hunt. I had ticked the box before I was forty, but that was all I did – ticked the box, once.

Chapter Seven

A Militant Cyclist's Tale

It is perhaps not surprising that the unexpected arrival at the traffic lights of the short bloke off *Top Gear* on a bicycle should elicit a response or two from car drivers. I have given this matter the benefit of my mediocre powers of thought on many occasions as I bare my knees and shed my dignity to cruise through London on my bike. But the simple fact is that a bicycle is the best mode of transport for getting about the place in a busy, congested city. Just because I work on the biggest TV car show in the world and am privileged to have access to the most expensive and exotic supercars available, I don't see why I should, as a result, be excluded from enjoying commuting to work by the most efficient means available to me. That it also serves to soothe the conscience of the soon-to-be-forty-year-old is, naturally, a welcome by-product.

By slinging a leg over the pushbike and enduring twenty minutes of pedal twirling at the beginning and end of my weekly *Top Gear* planning sessions at the BBC, I can tick the box marked 'Exercise' without having to suffer the misery of a trip to the gym with all the necessary stripping off in a crowded room full of muscle-bound twenty-year-olds and the shame of straining to lift weights adding up to a negligible fraction of the barbells and dumbbells those same twenty-year-olds swing about the place as easily as I might lift the glass I would far rather be lifting at that time of the evening. Nevertheless, it is not exactly a pleasant moment when I roll up to the lights and dab a foot to the floor to hold up my bicycle just in time for a chap in an expensive Audi to roll down the window and shout, 'Oi, where's the Ferrari, then?'

At moments like that, the bicycle clips burn twin rings of shame into my shins and the cycling helmet weighs pretty heavily on the old head, I can tell you. But I press on, clinging to my firm belief that the bicycle is the key not only to unlocking the congested streets but also to streamlining the queues of plumper individuals waiting in graffiti-laden bus stops to be collected by fume-spewing leviathans or waddling from expensive parking space to office desk and calling for doughnuts.

I would hesitate to say that I burst with pride each time I arrive at the BBC, sweating and draped in a fluorescent raincoat, but I will confess to enjoying a warm sense of wellbeing and of a job well done as I apply the lock to the metal steed and walk into the building on legs already benefiting from the exercise incurred during what would otherwise be a mundane and sedentary commute in a car that could not exceed twelve miles an hour, regardless of technical specification or price.

However, this pursuit of fitness and of – let us not try and convince ourselves otherwise – staving off the wear and tear associated with my rapidly approaching fortieth birthday does not always run as smoothly as might be hoped. On occasions I have, admittedly, squelched into the office and braced myself for an entirely justified barrage of hilarity from the assembled team following an early morning drenching in an unexpected cloudburst. On others, my arrival at the same office has been heralded by a warm and enveloping pong pouring forth from the lift as I enter the room to ask for the thousandth time why it is that those of us choosing to travel to work by the most politically correct and environmentally friendly mode of transport imaginable do not have access to showers in order to rid ourselves of the inevitable and entirely natural by-product of our exertions on arrival. But these issues are of no significance to the dedicated bicycle commuter.

I see a time when it will be possible for a man or woman to arrive at the office in bicycle clips and stride into the boardroom still streaked with rain and sweat and wear their puddle splashes and pungent odours with pride as badges of their commitment to the environment and to their own ongoing fitness. No: the problem with cycling to work comes when you start trying to look good doing it. It's not possible to look good when cycling to work, at least not in the eyes of those not cycling to work. And being someone off the telly excuses the cyclist not one minuscule drop of the shame and embarrassment headed their way the moment they even begin to think that they look anything other than a prize prat and a target for abuse and hilarity when aboard their steed.

I was perfectly happy in my weekly cycle commute. I would pull on cut-off gloves, crash helmet and jeans and hop aboard my little bike to set off for the office with not a care in the world. Apart, that is, from the cares about the fleets of buses that would try to kill me before I reached it. They do this on every trip and it is, I firmly believe, the drivers' favourite sport to see how much terror they can spread among the cycling fraternity. There is probably some secret, underground league table with points accrued by the drivers for their skill in cornering cyclists as they round turns, for pulling out on them just as they pass the bus at a bus stop and, without doubt, for executing the bus drivers' *coup de grâce* and placing themselves directly in front of the cyclist for as long as possible, forcing the rider to suck up more smoke than a jazz pianist in a windowless bar on a forty-eight-hour smoke 'n' jazz session.

But these trifling worries apart, I would set off from my little London flat, not heeding the catcalls from van drivers, the confused expressions on schoolchildren's faces and the murderous bus drivers' intent on racking up a few extra points at the expense of my lungs. And then one day, from nowhere, I grew self-conscious. This, too, is no doubt attributable to my forthcoming fortieth, but it is a nasty affliction for cycle commuters all the same and I hope that what follows might serve as a salutary tale to all who risk following me down the dark and dangerous path to bicyclist's vanity.

From nowhere, then, came this desire to 'smarten myself up a bit' for my weekly ride. Clearly, no tailor could fit me with a suit appropriate for the job, neither do even the very best of designer labels provide space on their rails for anything suitable for wearing by the cycling gentleman who is neither young nor old but wishes to comport himself in a manner not likely to trigger outright hilarity and derision on the part of bystanders and pedestrians. In short, I looked a proper numpty in my habitual outfit of knackered jeans, sweaty T-shirt, Converse trainers and cycling helmet and I wanted to up my game a bit in the biking fashion stakes.

It was a mistake, I know that now, and you can probably see this already, but I had not the benefit of hindsight at this point and I busied myself seeking clothes that might be acceptable on the busy streets when worn by a thirty-nine-year old bloke keen to blend in among the bright young things whizzing to work at a pace worthy of a slot in the Tour de France and still looking ready to drop into a nightclub to throw shapes or into a coffee shop to hold forth on matters philosophical and contemporary.

I opted to keep everything toned down. This might have been due to a lack of confidence or perhaps to an entirely appropriate mellowing of the desire to 'stand out' that characterized my youth. I selected a pair of black shorts; mid-length and made of a technical material of some sort that would, I was assured, allow my knees to 'sweat' if they so chose, they looked not at all bad in the shop. The T-shirt was a trickier one. I rejected tour T-shirts of any sort, reasoning that the choice of band displayed thereon would immediately send a statement out to the world of such authority and finality concerning my age, attitude and social placement that I could not bear to wrestle with the decision. I ordered one from a catalogue that dropped out of a motorcycle magazine. It was inexpensive but seemed well made, was grey and featured a Batman logo on the front. It was, I had no doubt, 'retro' and quite possibly 'ironic', too.

For the feet I chose a pair of really quite expensive trainers that rose up almost to cover the ankle and in so doing gave the impression of being technical bits of kit designed to offer just the specialized support and assistance demanded by chaps undertaking feats of physical endurance on a bicycle perhaps beyond the reach of lesser riders or of those whose age precluded them. The cycling helmet was, for this initial outing into the world as a suddenly stylish cyclist, my usual one. I am pleased, in fact, with my cycling helmet. Perhaps not surprisingly given my recent history with heads and injuries, I am quite fussy on the matter of protective headgear and I had already gone to great pains to select and always wear a decent example of the breed that promised much in the event of a calamity and, in the meantime, seemed to result in a not-entirely ridiculous effect visually.

On a dry, grey Tuesday morning, I assembled in the car park wearing the full rig and threw a leg over the bicycle ready to pedal into my new life as a stylish cyclist. It felt good knowing that I might not attract quite the same number of laughs, hoots and crude shouts to the effect that 'Jezza's got a Lamborghini, where's yours, then?' as I made my way to work.

And it had a genuinely soothing effect, this new-found confidence in my appearance. I felt calm, confident and assured. I cycled smoothly along the King's Road, turned left and headed for Earl's Court. Apart from one bloke in an air-conditioning firm's van asking if I'd sold the Porsche and another in a Mercedes SL giving me a funny look, London cared not a jot if Hammond wanted to cycle to work today. I reached the Warwick Road–Kensington High Street junction. This is a big junction and presents a daunting spread to the visiting cyclist. Buoyed up by my newly burnished confidence in my appearance, though, I rode confidently up to the bollards marking the borders of the junction. The traffic was dense and stood in four columns to my right. It was not a conscious decision, but I must have decided nonetheless, that I would try for the old 'see how long you can go without putting your feet down' routine displayed to great effect by cyclists on a daily basis at junctions just such as this.

The weak man or woman will ride up to such a point and resign themselves immediately to the inconvenience of unhooking a foot from the toe clips and dabbing it to the ground to support them while they wait for the lights to change. The next stage up is achieved by the cyclist who, in an opportunistic move reminiscent of carrion crows preying upon whatever they find already dead rather than risking all by killing it themselves, will cycle up to the junction, slow to a halt and then seek out some piece of street furniture against which they might rest a hand, thus removing from their journey the tiresome business of unhooking a foot from the pedal to support themselves until the light turns green and then fiddling about to reinsert foot in toe clip on departure.

The final category, though, is that occupied by the bravest and, I must admit, albeit reluctantly, most skilled of city cyclists. These are the players who cycle boldly to the front of the queue and then, apparently using magic or perhaps by dint of being in possession of gyroscopic ankles, manage to stand in the saddle and keep the bike upright, at a standstill, until the lights signal green, at which point, with feet still locked on to the pedals, they power away and leave the rest of the two-wheeled pack trailing dismally in their wake in a flurry of toe-clip fastening and gear selection. It can provide a magnificent spectacle when well executed and I decided, for reasons still not entirely clear to me, that this morning was my moment to step into the limelight at the head of the queue and dazzle London's commuters with a display of my own.

There is a small patch of tarmac reserved at the foot of the lights for cyclists. The purpose of this is clearly indicated by the painting, across this stretch, of a bicycle. This simple hieroglyphic still lacks sufficient clarity to keep some of London's van-hefting population from parking in the middle of it, but I was pleased on this, of all mornings, to find the patch of tarmac free of vans and, apart from one lowly example on a mountain bike and wearing jeans and a suit jacket, of cyclists. I entered the hallowed zone gingerly, for this stretch of reserved tarmac is that most likely to be frequented by one of London's talented young bicycle hoverers. I kept my speed as low as I felt prudent, still making for the empty space in a confident manner, but anxious to spend as much of the red light period of the traffic light's sequence moving rather than in my first ever hover. As the rear wheel broached the borders of the patch reserved for bicycles, I looked up at the traffic lights. They remained resolutely red and, from the rush of traffic running perpendicular to my own path, I figured would stay red for some time yet. I would have to hover.

I raised myself up off the seat. I had never tried this, but I had watched in fascination as it was done and felt sure that I had the imagination and visualisation skills needed to feel my way through the exercise based only on my visual assessment of it. Turning the bars is the key; I turned them firmly and smoothly, applying a little pedal pressure, easing back on the brakes to hold the forward motion and turning the bars a little to counter any lean as soon as it started. And it worked. I kept the bike, if not at a stationary hover, then advancing at a rate of about a foot an hour. I risked another look up to the lights, adopting the same impatient posture I have seen displayed by the cyclists I had previously admired carrying out exactly the manoeuvre I was now performing in front of a crammed stream of waiting traffic at the lights leading across the busy Kensington High Street. As I eased the bike forwards another inch and felt the resistance through the brake lever, the lights changed to green and the onward rush began. With both feet already locked on to the pedals and the correct gear pre-selected

137

in my hovering manoeuvre, I was ready to go instantly and hit the power in order to stay ahead of the thunderous charge now gathering pace behind me.

I knew that I would have to give way from the centre of the road where I now rode and I began a slow drift across to the left. Barely two metres across Kensington High Street, though, a problem presented itself. And it seemed like a large and insurmountable one. I could pedal no further and the bicycle freewheeled to a halt. My right leg moved out from the pedal and tried to counterbalance a terminal lean to the left. Instinctively, I threw my left leg out to stop me from falling. But my left foot would not come away from the pedal. The lean to the left was increasing now and it was inevitable that I would fall. And I did. Without moving my left foot off the pedal, I fell to the left, hitting the road with my shoulder, my knee and soon after, my pelvis. My left foot was still clamped to the pedal.

Strangely, even though it wasn't welded to the bars in the manner that my left foot had suddenly become welded to the pedal, I didn't so much as lift my left hand from the grip to save my fall. With my left foot still stuck to the pedal and now the entire assembly jammed under the stricken bicycle and kept there by my own body weight, I could not stand up and so I sort of squirmed and wriggled across the road to the gutter with the bike still jammed between my legs. There was a lot of hooting and shouting. A man on a bicycle said something that was indistinct but in a tone that was enough to inform me was quite rude.

With no alternative, I reached down to my left foot, my hand running between the crossbar and down tube of the bike's frame, to try and investigate this sudden fixing of my left foot. Very quickly, I discovered what had happened. During my hovering manoeuvre, perhaps, the lace of my fashionably technical shoe had come undone and fallen into the 'rat-trap' of the pedal and had then wrapped itself around the spindle of the pedal itself. After just two or three rotations of the crank, the lace had wound itself as tight as it could go and the system had jammed. My foot was effectively tied to the pedal and unable to go forwards any more. And I had fallen off.

The T-shirt was a great hit at the office. I received several positive comments on it during the day. The shoes, though, were less of a success and the subject of several disapproving glances. They have gone in the bin. And I cycle to work still, but wearing jeans, ordinary trainers, bicycle clips, a helmet and a Batman T-shirt. And I've learned to ignore what people say.

Chapter Eight

The Question

It was one of those important moments, an instant drenched in significance and meaning when The Question changed. I don't recall the actual moment itself; it may have been in a multi-storey car park in Cheltenham or it may have been on a street corner in London. Wherever and whenever, though, there came the moment when The Question changed. By 'The Question', I mean the one asked of me on first meeting anyone, anywhere, anytime. Traditionally, and of course, not surprisingly, this has for some time been, 'So what's the best car you've ever driven?' The actual form of words might vary slightly; The Question might be prefaced by a bit of embarrassed collar-tugging and a spot of 'I know you must get asked this all the time', or 'I'm sorry, I'm sure you're sick of being asked this', but, whatever the specific wording, the content would amount to precisely the same enquiry. It might be asked by a confident young lad in a lift, a charming old man in a barber's shop or – and this has happened – a slightly too-familiar dentist looming at me in the chair with a pair of pliers and wearing a face mask.

I had grown rather fond of The Question. It brought with it a sort of familiarity and became for me the modern equivalent of the formal greetings exchanged by strangers in bygone times. On first encountering someone at a party or outside the school gates, there was no need for me to scratch around for some topic of conversation. I could simply prepare an answer to The Question, fire it off at the appropriate moment and then follow it up with a second volley which was a simple enquiry concerning the best car my interrogator has ever driven. Perfect: all social awkwardness neatly side-stepped, conversation warmly begun and a warm and friendly atmosphere sloshing about the place; everybody wins.

But then there was a change. I might encounter someone in the street or a hotel lobby and, as I mentally sifted through and selected from a range of stock answers to The Question, this stranger would approach, cough politely and deliver an entirely different question. It wrong-footed me on several occasions and it wasn't until midway through a pretty in-depth speech concerning how the potential advantages in terms of reliability and mechanical durability brought by a Pagani Zonda's largely Mercedes drive train might have been edged into second place by the recent involvement of Audi with Lamborghini, that I would realise that they hadn't asked me to tell them what the best car I have ever driven is. What they had just delivered, as I would realise later, was

The New Question. And this one ran thus: 'Did you really [insert ridiculous moment from *Top Gear*] or was it made up for the telly?'

You will have gathered, then, that The New Question contains within it a substantial part that can change with each instance of it being asked; namely the bit in the middle where the questioner mentions a specific incident from *Top Gear*. It's a seasonal thing; it changes. For roughly a quarter of a year, maybe more, The New Question was, 'Were you really chased out of town by those American rednecks, or was it made up for the telly?' This referred to an incident in a programme we made while trying to find out if it was possible to buy a car and drive across a chunk of the USA for less money than the traditional 'fly-drive' schemes offered by the holiday companies. It's a pretty lengthy story and I shan't recount it all here but in the course of our trip we had, by way of an entertaining diversion to keep up our spirits during an especially lengthy drive, devised a plan whereby we would each try and get the others killed. It was a pretty nifty idea, in fact.

We would each decorate the other's vehicle with slogans that we felt might stir the feelings of the locals, cause maximum discomfort to the driver and, of course, raise a laugh for the viewer at home. And so, in a broad, dusty lay-by at the side of a road leading to Alabama, we parked up and set to with the paint brushes, spray cans and stencils. On the side of Jeremy's ageing, beaten up Trans Am I painted the legend, 'Country Music is Rubbish'. I figured that this statement, daubed in lurid pink poster-paint down the side of a clearly abused and mistreated American sports car might just insert itself up the noses of the flag-waving, banjo-twanging residents of Alabama.

Jeremy had adorned the flanks of James's 1970s Cadillac with 'Hillary for President' and 'Nascar Sucks' – a reference to Nascar racing which is, he assured me, pretty much a religion in the Deep South. I laughed at the slogans with Jeremy as we stood under the tall, smooth-barked trees and sheltered from the Southern sun. James was still finishing the lettering on the side of my white pick-up truck and I didn't want to spoil the moment by peeking before his work was done. Eventually, with a confident flourish of the brush and a grin, the significance of which would only register with me later, James indicated that he had completed his masterpiece and was happy for us to step up and survey it. We stepped up and surveyed.

Along the side of my white pick-up truck, James had painted – with characteristic precision – just four short words: 'Man Love Rules OK'.

Well, fair enough: it was perhaps the strongest of our three examples of automotive artwork, but nevertheless we all felt that we would cause, at worst, a ripple of offence no more deeply felt than might be generated among the residents of Cornwall by three visitors choosing to drive their cars through Truro with 'Cream Teas Are Rubbish' painted down the side. The plan now was simple: with the slogans complete, saddle up and head off through Alabama en route for Louisiana. It even sounded cool as it rolled off the tongue. We saddled up and headed off. We covered three miles before being placed in genuine fear of our lives.

Things started well enough. We pulled out of the lay-by, swung on to what even James had started calling the 'highway' by now, and rumbled towards the border with Alabama. The road was broad and empty, with a single carriageway in each direction, and was fringed by dark-fronded trees with grey trunks and heavy branches hanging over us. Our convoy included the three cars being filmed and, naturally, the cars and jeeps carrying the film crew and their equipment. It was a very hot day, and every vehicle travelled with windows down and its occupants' elbows out – not least James, since Jeremy and I had disabled his air-conditioning system with a crowbar at a campsite the previous evening. We were obliged to keep things at an amiable cruising pace, principally by the local speed limits, of course, but also by the limitations of James's monster Caddie in the motive department; he had chosen a very big car with a very small amount of power.

After just a mile or two, we spotted a road sign telling us that we were in Alabama and pulled over to film it. The sign was riddled with bullet holes. And not the pathetic little air rifle pellet holes you might occasionally see punctuating the lettering across such a sign in the UK; this thing was peppered with shotgun blasts and a few larger, gaping wounds inflicted, I could only imagine as I stared at the jagged bullet holes on the back of the thing, by slugs from high-powered hunting rifles. We were definitely not in Cornwall. The cicadas turned up their frantic chirping in the dense woodland beyond the verges and we sloped back to our vehicles in silence, scuffing our boots across the dusty verge and looking out from under our sun hats and baseball caps at the cool depths of the woods. The coolness would doubtless be a welcome relief from the fierce heat, but what else would we discover if we ventured out there? Best not to enquire.

A mile or so later, we pulled into what Jeremy seemed keen to call a 'gas station' to buy, one could only imagine, some gas. They also sold petrol, which was handy because a number of us were in danger of running dry. James, Jeremy and I pulled up in front of three rusty fuel pumps on the forecourt and heaved our sweating bodies out of our cars and into the merciless heat, grateful at least for some shade under the forecourt canopy. The crew cars pulled up in a line to one side of us and I saw doors opening slowly as the guys weighed up the desirability of a can of cold Coke bought from the kiosk against the misery of a hot trudge under the sun's furnace to get it. Nothing could move quickly on a day like this. Nothing.

As I rested a hand on the hot metal of the petrol pump nozzle and readied myself to heave it up and slot it into the car, a movement across the forecourt made me stop. A woman, a local presumably, was walking towards us. She had a long, rangy frame, and looked to be made of wire and gristle underneath the plaid shirt and jeans. Maybe fifty years old with yellowing hair and brown teeth.

'Y'all queers trying to see how long you can last in a hick town?' Her voice was loud and so nasal you could feel it in your own chest.

'Ah, er ...' I looked across at Jeremy who was staring at the woman. James frowned, trying, I guessed, to penetrate her thick accent.

I felt a response was appropriate but was keen not to bait the woman. She looked frighteningly tough. I could imagine her sustaining a prolonged attack from troops and helicopter gunships and still getting back up like a zombie to exact revenge on her attackers for criticising her meat loaf.

'No.' I smiled in a soothing, friendly way as I spoke and I dared a few cautious steps away from the pumps towards the questioner. There was more movement around us on the forecourt now. Trucks were arriving and in the back of them I saw the broad backs and cowboy hats of what I could only imagine were more locals. Where they had sprung from I had no idea. But I saw that they were all carrying guns, propped up against their feet on the floor of their pick-ups. And I suddenly wanted to be away from here. More voices had joined in now and those voices were hardening and growing fiercer. I tried to make my own sound friendly, yet confident – manly even, though soothing. I addressed the woman as one might a panther when cornered up a tree.

'No, look, we're both married. Got kids. Just travelling through.' I pointed a finger at Jeremy across the other side of a fuel pump from where I stood.

'Yup,' he chimed in. 'Got kids. Travelling through.'

An enormous man had come out of the station building now to stand in the middle of the forecourt, seemingly occupying most of it. He wore the regulation blue denim overalls, plaid shirt and work boots of a cartoon character and looked like you couldn't stop him with a train locomotive. He drew in a breath so vast that it threatened to take in the pump nozzles, fire buckets and newspaper stand with it and he looked around at us from under a brow with an overhang to challenge a rock climber. In an unexpectedly high voice, he started to count.

'Ten. Nine ...' He may have been counting the numbers off on his fingers – in fact he probably was – but I didn't stop to look. The crew cars were actually coming under attack now. A group of locals had assembled in a ragtag line and were throwing rocks at them. I heard them land loudly against the hollow, metal sides of the kit van. I watched as those members of the crew who had decided to brave the heat for the promise of a cool drink in the petrol station regretted their decision and ran back to their vehicles. The cameramen had been set up ready to film us filling the cars before setting off again. Instead, they were transformed suddenly into war correspondents, filming now while the gang of locals threw rocks at them.

'Er, Hammond.' James had come into view and, just as he stepped up, I could see, over his shoulder, Jeremy's blue Trans Am fire up and head for the road with a screech of tyres.

'I need a jump-start again, I'm afraid.' The battery on James's gargantuan Caddy had faded over the previous two days and it had become a matter of routine to pull up alongside him in my pick-up truck, hoist the bonnet, hook up the jump leads and give his car a boost to get the creaky old engine turning. It was not a matter of routine, however, to go through this involved process while a growing crowd of local rednecks threw rocks at us and shouted with murderous intent while others waved shotguns over the backs of their pick-ups.

'Seven …' The man mountain on the forecourt was still counting. It was taking a while – I suspect he may have been operating at the very limit of his abilities as he did so – but something about his dull, heavy tones suggested that when he did make it back from ten down to zero, something pretty awful would happen.

'Shit. Not now.' But there was no choice. 'Right, you get ready. I'm coming over.'

The Caddie was about twenty metres away across the forecourt and James ran back to it. By the time he had reached it, got in and pulled the bonnet release, I was parked alongside.

'Five.' The counter was still going slowly, still struggling with the number sequence but he gave no sign that he was about to give up and I didn't have time to think about what happened at zero.

I leapt out of the truck, pulling the bonnet release on the way and grabbed the jump leads as James thrust them towards me. Hauling the bonnet up with one arm, I had the first clip on to the battery terminal instantly and hurled myself under the bonnet of the Caddie to connect one, then the other lead before returning to the pick-up and connecting the last.

'Three.'

The hail of rocks on to the crew vehicles was intensifying as the drivers came to their senses, started up and retreated.

'Get in, James. Turn it over.' I had left the truck running. The old Caddie gave a heave and the engine made a couple of wheezing turns before it caught and fired up, settling into a lumpen but determined stagger. I ripped the cables out of its engine bay and slammed the bonnet shut.

'Two.'

'Go go go.' I spun round, tore the cable out from the pick-up's battery and slammed the bonnet shut. It was still running and so was the Caddie. I couldn't hear the man counting now. He must have reached zero and as I threw myself into the cab I expected to be enveloped in a mushroom cloud at any moment. Before the door was shut I had stamped on the clutch and thrown it into gear. The wheels chirruped on the hot tarmac as I turned to the right and slewed the truck on to the road. The crew had made it to their cars now and our cavalcade moved off in a ragged line. More rocks landed around us as we pulled away. Voices burst in an excited rush from the CB radio as those not driving or filming through car windows checked in with the rest of our convoy.

'What the hell was that about?'

'Dunno. Just leave. Leave. We've got to go.'

'We're gonna die. They're gonna kill us.'

'Think I shit meself.' Iain 'Flash' May exclaimed, doubtless still grinning as he caught the action through his viewfinder.

Grabbing third gear and keeping my boot nailed to the floor to squeeze every last ounce of go from the truck as our retreat gained pace, I saw the trucks from the garage pulling away. In the back of each one, sitting square against the sides of the pick-up bed in sombre lines, the rednecks toted their shotguns, thin black barrels bristling straight up at the sky past their broad shoulders. Among the tense squabble of English voices from our team crackling across the CB, I heard the slow drawl of a local.

'They're comin' up past here. We're at the crossroads.' Some trucks had left before us, tearing up the road to God only knew where.

'I can see them here, too.'

They were using their CB radios to track us. And I was suddenly very much aware that TV cameras and business cards would not protect us from guns carried by people quite prepared, from what I had seen so far, to use them. I didn't want to wake up tied to a tree being invited to squeal like a little piggy for the morbid entertainment of some twenty-year-old psychopath in giant dungarees with three teeth in his head and a bitter hatred of anyone who wasn't also a thirty-stone, homophobic racist who shot at things he didn't understand simply because he didn't understand them.

It was all on TV. You may have seen it. A few miles down the road, conscious that we were easily identifiable to the hordes of rednecks being warned of our approach over the CB, we pulled over. We had seen them waiting at crossroads as we passed, and heard them telling people further ahead that we were coming. We had to try and remove the slogans that had caused offence of an intensity way beyond what we had anticipated. We timed the stop using the CB radio, agreeing quickly that pulling over as a unit in a cavalcade some ten cars strong gave us extra security. Our wheels had barely stopped turning before key members of the crew threw themselves out of their vehicles and ran over to the three presenters' cars, tore off their T-shirts, soaked them in water from bottles and began wiping frantically at the painted words. I joined them. Breathlessly, as we scrubbed, we spoke of the danger, the fear and the sheer wildness and strangeness of people reacting in this way. One cameraman – inevitably it was Iain 'Flash' May – had both the presence of mind and lunacy to film us on his mobile phone. The footage would later be inserted into the finished film.

Some of the paint was harder to remove, but we needed to get all of it off if we were to stand a chance of getting out of Alabama without causing further offence and attracting more locals. When we ran out of bottled water, we used soft drinks instead, ripping the tabs off the cans and pouring the contents on to T-shirts before continuing to scrub at the stubborn paint. Weirdly, a lone police car drew up and cruised the length of our convoy as we worked. It didn't stop and we peered through the dark windows to see who was rolling past for a slow-speed inspection of these half-naked strangers wiping frantically at the dusty flanks of their cars. The presence of the police car did nothing to dispel the fear that now tugged at every one of us.

The fear slowly subsided as we drove out of Alabama.

But we kept going. And, years later, The New Question is still asked of me, 'Did that really happen in America at the petrol station, or did you make it up for the telly?' Well, yes, it really happened. Ask anyone who was there.

Of course, the whole point of The New Question is that it can take many forms. 'Did you really cross the Channel in a pick-up truck, or did you make it all up for the telly?' Answer: yes, we did. It was a very long way and people were quite surprised on the beach when we arrived in a truck. 'Did James really strip off to drive that Aston on the way to the Stelvio Pass?' Yes, unfortunately, he did. Not an agreeable memory but I feel, nevertheless, obliged to report faithfully and honestly, even if it means the odd trip into dim corners of my mind that are best left to fester undisturbed.

And I really don't mind The New Question. After all, if people feel compelled to question whether some feat or event in one of our programmes could ever have been done for real, then it follows that they must be at least slightly impressed. I would say, in fact, that I prefer The New Question to the old one.

It does begin to grate a little, though, when The New Question turns upon some physical feat of endurance undertaken, usually, by me. And so when there was a brief period during which it became fashionable to ask me 'Did you really beat the other two in that race across London when they were on a speedboat and in a car and you were on a bicycle, or did you just make it up?' I developed an instinctive flinch and learned to grind my teeth a little and clench my jaw before answering. I think the reason for my sensitivity to this particular form of The New Question is founded upon the simple reasoning that, having undergone whatever physical challenge I am being questioned about, be it running to the North Pole or cycling across London, all in the name of making a TV programme, it is pretty galling to feel that people watching the end result of that effort harbour a suspicion that I was actually loafing about on a sofa in a studio in front of a green screen the whole time.

Of course, there is a further complication: When the feat concerned is one requiring physical endurance, fitness and toughness, it immediately crashes into the tangled and treacherous territory of my approach to forty. A chap becomes a bit squeamish and jumpy about the idea that he might not be up to some physical challenge or other as he nears middle age; and so, when I am asked if I really did win the race on a bicycle against a speed-boat and a car, I'll admit to experiencing a strong urge to respond to the question by asking, 'What, don't think I'm up to it? Too old? Past it?' I don't give voice to this urge, obviously. But I think it, every time.

We had set out to prove what I guess we all kind of suspected all along anyway: that the fastest mode of transport across London and, indeed, pretty much any city, is the bicycle. When the idea was first floated about the office, I was only too keen to get involved. I generally use a bicycle to get around London anyway and this would be a chance to champion what is, I believe, a truly wonderful mode of transport.

In the event, I made a few significant mistakes in the

planning stages. For one thing, I left the choice of clothing and kit to the production team. Inevitably, then, I turned up on the day to find that, while they had equipped me with a wonderfully hi-tech bicycle, complete with carbon-fibre frame and about a million gears, I would be riding it wearing a pair of baggy shorts and a clammy, gut-clinging T-shirt of such an intense and violent yellow that I feared I might trigger some pre-rehearsed response from the city's emergency teams to chemical attack or spillage.

The race would start at Kew Bridge and take us through London by whatever route was most appropriate to our respective forms of transport and on to the finish at London's City Airport. It was a distance, for me anyway, of some twenty miles: easy to achieve, though, in my case certainly, tricky to do so stylishly. When the word was given and we started the race, James sauntered off to his comfortable, spacious Mercedes, Jeremy trotted down to the river to climb into a speedboat powerful enough to tow all the bridges of London into one big heap at the end and I threw a skinny white leg over the bicycle and wobbled off into town looking like an underfed pizza delivery boy.

I won – pedalling furiously up the final stretches before throwing the bike into the racks and hobbling into the airport concourse, a sweaty but victorious mess. My elation was somewhat diminished when I learned that we would now, having completed and filmed a real-time run of the race in order to establish the genuine result, be obliged to go back over the route and pick up any shots that had been impossible to get under race conditions. As I leaned on the counter of the coffee shop and sucked up a third glass of water, I asked the director for clarification on this point. What it amounted to, as far as I could make out over the blood pulsing through my ears like thunder, was that I would now ride the route again, only this time for another set of cameras that would be waiting at various points along the way.

I rode the route again, recreating the sections that would have been impossible to film the first time without interrupting the race and contaminating the results. Once again, I pumped furiously along the roads leading to the airport and arrived at the doors with legs throbbing so hard I expect bystanders could hear them. I handed the bike to a technician who busied himself checking the onboard cameras and recording units strapped to its spindly frame while I hauled my own spindly frame back up to the airport lounge, where I called for a trough of water to drink, and another and another. A short while later, as I battled manfully to slake a thirst strong enough to draw water from sand, the technician appeared next to me at the counter. He had the nervous air of a man about to pop his head in a tiger's mouth for a bet.

'Ah, now, you okay?'

I dipped the glass briefly to inform him that, yes, I was okay. And I waited for him to come to whatever point it was that was clearly troubling him. There was a pause during which I sucked up another pint of water and called to the attendant to replenish my glass. The technician watched with haunted eyes. Then he swelled his small chest with a mighty breath and blurted out:

'The tapes didn't work.'There was another pause, quite a long one. I turned over in my mind various quips and barbed comments, rejecting them all in favour of a more direct and immediate response.

'Sorry, you what?'

'The tapes didn't work. Not for all of it, only the last bit.'

'The last bit.'

'The last bit, yes. Problem with the heads. Or something. And the funny thing is, well, not funny obviously, but the thing is, they didn't work for that bit on the first run either. I've fixed it now though, but …'

'But I'll have to do it again.'

'Well, only the last bit.'

'The last bit.'

'Yes, that. Just from the roundabout at the bottom of the hill.'

'At the bottom of the hill.'

'Yes, from there.'

I make no claims at the best of times for being a man in possession of an especially rapier-like intellect, but I was having trouble by even my own limited standards with grasping what the man was getting at.

'So, the tapes didn't work on my second go and now I have to do it again?'

'Yes. But only …'

'Only the last bit.'

'Yes.'

'The hill up to the airport.'

'Yes, that.'

'The hill.'

We were in danger of being stuck in an eternal exchange. I hobbled off mutely, found the bike, strained to persuade shrinking tendons and cramping muscles to comply and allow my throbbing leg back over it before settling gingerly into the saddle once more and repeating the final few miles of the run, confident that this time the cameras would be running and capture my ruddy face during the moments of exquisite pain and exertion.

They did, it was on the telly; you may have seen it. And so, in response to what was for a while the fashionable version of The New Question: yes, I did ride the bike across London and, yes, I did win. Oh, and if you were wondering about the answer to The Question that preceded The New Question, the best car I've ever driven is my worthless old Land Rover, across a field, with two dogs, my daughters and my wife in it, all heading for a picnic and a lazy afternoon.

Chapter Nine

Around the World with *Top Gear Live*

'The thing is, how many careers would any of us have to live through before one of them involves the chance to go on a world tour with a massive stage show and get paid for it?' I nodded my head to emphasise the words as I spoke, finished with a flourish and sank back into the sofa. Smiling triumphantly, I slurped my tea, suddenly conscious that tea wasn't very rock and roll right now, given the conversation Jeremy and I had been having in the greenroom at Johannesburg's Coca-Cola Dome. The pinball machine let out a sudden stream of jangling trills in an attempt to lure one of us back across the room to its spangly temptations. Outside, somewhere in the cavernous, concrete-walled compound of the stadium, an engine revved frantically: one of the stunt guys getting their crazily fast Rage buggy warmed up, ready for the next show.

We had been well looked after on this trip, with a greenroom packed full of everything the organisers felt we could possibly need to keep us happy: so mostly crisps, bowls of sweets, a pinball machine with a pirate ship on it and a fridge full of Red Bull. But I now assumed this to be part of a calculated attempt to persuade us to take the show further afield, for longer on a more elaborate and far-reaching tour. We had already taken our car-based stage show to London and Birmingham and now were finishing up in South Africa. But this, under discussion, was a full-blown world tour. We were talking multiple continents here.

This, we could pretty safely declare, was Big.

Jeremy smiled and nodded his agreement with my theory on careers and world tours. I suspected that he had already considered the possibility of a such a trip for our *Top Gear Live* show long before Chris, the boss of the events company organising the show, had stumbled into our greenroom, helped himself to a Red Bull from our fridge, adjusted his round, metal-framed glasses and asked if we fancied touring the show properly next year. He spoke excitedly of coming back to South Africa and then going on to Australia, New Zealand, Hong Kong, Dublin and God knows where else. And his excitement was genuine and heartfelt; he might have been in it for a good few years, but he still enjoyed this business more, I suspected, than anyone else in our huge team. He had left now, bustling off to tend to some technical, political or, more likely, financial aspect of the show elsewhere in the cavernous dome. He's probably the funniest man I know, capable of flights of fancy and fantasy that leave you breathless not only with laughter but with admiration for his creative abilities. If Jeremy and I arrived at whatever stadium or theatre was hosting the show in a particular city with massive hangovers and eye bags like a fortnight's luggage, it was generally because Chris had taken us out the night before and got carried away, turning a casual drink into a full-bore, headlong charge into oblivion. And if the man running the show asks his performers to come out for a drink, well, they can hardly say no, can they?

This was the second time we had brought our show to South Africa, although my memories of the first visit were limited. It had been in early 2007 and was the first work I was allowed to do after coming out of hospital, following a certain car crash. I had begged and pleaded with the doctors to let me go, reasoning that I was in danger of turning myself into a full-time and permanent patient if I didn't take the plunge and get back into my world soon. Reluctantly, they agreed to let me go, but only if provision was made for me to have a lie-down in between shows, and only if I made a solemn promise not to get tangled up going out of an evening with the crew – I was still not allowed to drink anything alcoholic at that point. A bed was provided in a darkened room back-stage, full-time, permanent medical support was made available and I was given strict instructions to speak up if I felt anything untoward. I suspect, though, that it really was too soon, a suspicion borne out now by the fact that I cannot actually remember the trip at all. Of ten days spent in Johannesburg performing a live stage show three or four times a day in front of audiences of three or four thousand people, all I can remember is driving onstage in some sort of really big truck and saying 'hello' into a microphone. But the show had gone well and we were back now for a second visit and suggesting a third as part of the proposed 'World Tour'. Much fun had been had earlier in the week when Chris and Jeremy discovered my inability to remember the previous trip. By the end of the first day, they had assured me that I had performed the entire show in drag and then done a nightly turn in a lap-dancing joint. And now, four days later, still not an opportunity was missed to point out some other aspect of the previous trip that had slipped my poor, battered mind. The game had extended further among the crew and all manner of costumes, acts, liaisons and carrying-on had been attributed to me on the now infamous last trip. And it's exactly that sort of arsing about that made the idea of a proper world tour so appealing.

*

'I mean, it's got to be done.' I chucked a sugar into my tea with a casual flourish in what I felt might be a more devil-may-care, rock'n'roll fashion. Our next show that day was due to start in half an hour. Fifteen minutes from now, the sound technician would arrive bearing a tray with three sets of earplugs and microphones. The third presenter with Jeremy and me was Sasha Martinengo, a South African radio host and motor sports commentator who gave the show much-needed local content and humour and who had slotted into our team readily and quickly. He had been with us on our first trip to Jo'burg and was now very much part of the family. He wasn't in the greenroom with us when Chris arrived and popped the question about the world tour, though; he was away conducting yet another interview with local journalists. The show's arrival in Jo'burg was a big deal; tickets were sold out. People travelled hundreds of miles to come and see the three of us goof about onstage, argue about which country had the worst weather, laugh at each other's attempts at building cars, race each other around the arena in a variety of ludicrous creations and introduce stunt driving sequences from experts capable of such precision and accuracy behind the wheel that it was sometimes difficult to take the wheel ourselves and strut our own limited abilities in front of a paying audience. Still, if it went wrong we could always fall over and make a joke of it. The whole atmosphere was relaxed, informal and fun. And that's what people wanted to see.

Sasha came back and we talked about the show we were about to do. Having already performed it, in slightly different guises, some twenty times in London and Birmingham, Jeremy and I were familiar enough with it to walk out pretty much on autopilot. The only danger came from all of us, drivers, presenters, stuntmen, dancers and stage crew, growing complacent and forgetting the obvious things. After another cup of tea and a quick run-through with Jeremy and Sasha of who had to remember to do what and say what and when, the technician arrived with our kit and we got ready to go onstage. The earplugs we wore were of the type used by real rock and roll performers in huge stadium shows. They were custom-built for the users by a man who visited us each at home and squirted rubber stuff into our ears to take a mould. The plugs themselves fitted perfectly, but took some jamming into our ears. Jeremy was hopping about now, jamming an earplug into his left ear with his thumb, grimacing with the effort and imploring his ear to stop messing about and just take it like a man. I picked up the silvery wires of my set, the clear, plastic plugs dangling from the ends. And suddenly, another rare memory came hurtling back, gleaming and intact, from the previous year's trip. I had worn exactly the same plugs, but the South African heat and our perhaps less than exacting standards of attentiveness to the business of cleaning and disinfecting them after every show, had, inevitably, led to me getting an infection in my ear. The problem had worsened as the infection took hold and was doubtless further agitated by my repeatedly jamming the earplug back in and feeding loud noises through it directly on to the inflamed and tender eardrum for an hour and a half, three times a day. On the penultimate morning, I was complaining to Chris, in a casual, inconsequential manner, of a headache. A bit cruel of me really, given his situation as the impresario of a show that was reintro-ducing me to work after I'd been brain-damaged only six months earlier. Chris winced and showed concern. Was I okay to carry on? Did I want to sit this next show out? Should he get the special medic? I assured him that, no, I didn't and would be fine. As I turned away from him, I glanced back to see the colour drain from his face. His right hand came up towards me.

'Er, mate, er, what's that?' He pointed to my left ear, his

eyes now huge behind his glasses. I lifted my own hand to my infected ear and dabbed at it with a finger. The digit came away smeared with blood. The infection had obviously burst in some way.

'Oh, I've just got a problem with my ...' I began to explain that it was an ear infection before the significance of what Chris had seen hit me. Blood was now coming out of the ear of a recently rather famously brain-damaged performer in his show. I rather suspect that Chris, at that exact moment, very nearly ruptured something inside his own head. It took quite a lot of explaining, reassuring and comforting to establish that, no, my brain was not suddenly choosing to leak out of my ear; no, Chris was not about to be sued for millions by my soon-to-be widow; and, no, he had not inadvertently killed a member of our tight-knit little travelling family with his greed and ambition. Personally, I thought it bloody hilarious at the time and relished every second of his misery and discomfort. Nature got its own back, though; my infected eardrum burst on the flight home, which meant twelve hours spent perching on my seat, cupping my left ear and whimpering at the attendants for more painkillers.

I smiled and winced at the returning memory and jammed the exact same earplug into my now-healed left ear before setting off with the lads for the stage and the roar of another crowd.

✳

In just a week's time I would be setting off for a month-long trip around the world. This was it, the *Top Gear Live* World Tour. It had indeed seemed like a great idea at the time. But it seemed like a bloody terrible one right now, as I contemplated leaving home and Mindy and our girls for a full month. Whenever I've got a big trip coming up, we sort of turn up the wick on doing family stuff for a week or so before I go. This was a big trip, so we had been making a big effort to do fun, family stuff together on this occasion. As part of this agenda, I had arranged to go horse riding with Mindy. Of course, I would need a horse, having sold mine a few years back because I was never there to ride it. I made great claims at the time that this was because it is cruel to keep but not ride a horse and that they soon get out of condition and lose their edge. I had owned the horse for over a year and only ridden it twice. This, I claimed, would make him unhappy and unfulfilled so he must be rehoused with someone better able to keep him content. Secretly, this was actually because I had worked out what the thing cost me per mile and realised it would be cheaper to run a Ferrari. Interestingly, I did subsequently buy a Ferrari, an elderly 550 Maranello. And, no, it wasn't cheaper to run than the horse, not by a very, very long way.

And so now, horseless but keen to share with Mindy a lifelong passion of hers before I departed on my tour, we made an appointment at a local equestrian place to borrow a horse and ride out on it at the weekend. I would need to try it first so we set off for the stables, helmets at the ready. We didn't go in the Ferrari, incidentally.

It was broken. It always is. We went instead in Mindy's Land Rover. Which never breaks down because, in order for something to break down it first has to function properly. On arriving at the stables, we were met by a pleasant, horsey gent wearing an appropriate flat cap and tweed jacket. He went to fetch the beast while Mindy and I tooled up and made ready to test it out. The pleasant horsey chap returned, dragging behind him a lead rope, attached to the end of which was an old blanket and some kitchen chairs. On closer inspection, this turned out to be the horse I was there to test. I fiddled with the zipper on my jacket and glanced surreptitiously around at the empty, sand riding school lying in the gentle, early spring warmth to my left. So I wouldn't be making a fine and heroic spectacle anytime soon. At least nobody would see. Well, there were a couple of sturdy women plodding about the yard on equally sturdy nags but they had the look of horsey women who had seen it all before and would take a great deal of impressing by anyone on horseback.

'Righto, then, here goes. Er,' I stood next to the horse, which turned out to answer to the name of Thomas. Well, I say 'answer to the name of'; he really didn't look likely to answer to the name of anything in a hurry anytime soon, unless perhaps a gentle tap on the shoulder and a discreet but urgent cough from his maker. Still, this was important to Mindy; we would ride out together the following day and share splendid times indulging in a pastime so laden with romantic associations in her mind that she probably wouldn't even notice that I was lumbering along beside her riding what looked, from some angles, to be a mobile jumble sale with a tail. Thomas looked down at me. At a little over fifteen hands, he wasn't a big beast, but he had a big, long head. And a surprisingly dim face. I raised a hand to stroke his velvety nostrils. He sneezed into my palm and fixed me with a stare from his dull, stony eye.

'We're gonna get on just fine,' I breathed in what I was certain Mindy would take to be a manly, Horse Whisperer kind of way. Containing her desire, Mindy responded by busying herself asking questions of the pleasant horsey chap about Thomas. I failed to listen, being preoccupied squinting to see if, from any angle at all, I could make a remotely dashing image on board Thomas's broad, sagging back. Probably not, I concluded. Thomas raised his head to look longingly at a field of grass beyond the yard and farted loudly. I blushed under my riding hat, sure that no one would attribute the roaring outburst to me, but nevertheless made slightly awkward by it having come from anyone in our little group, just as one might feel in a lift. Though not, it should be said, in a lift with a large, Welsh cob called Thomas who turned out to have intestinal workings modelled on a post-accident Chernobyl.

The time came to do some actual riding. While Thomas and I had got on with the business of forming that ancient and mystical bond between man and horse, and doing a lot of farting – both of us guffing away merrily by now, I must confess, as the opportunity to surreptitiously release a little gas when there's someone there for all to blame is one never to be passed up – Mindy had walked across the yard with the pleasant horsey chap and selected another horse so that she could ride out with me on my test drive and assess for herself the suitability, or otherwise, of my potential charger. The usual clatter of hooves heralded her arrival aboard a smart little bay hunter, all trim and composed. She drew the horse up alongside me, its compact form suggesting contained and controllable energy. I looked at Thomas. He managed not to fart, but did sag a bit in the middle.

'Right then, could I have a hand up please …?' I wobbled my shoulders about a bit to emphasise my hopelessness to the pleasant horsey chap, who had returned on foot behind Mindy, having sorted her out with her gleaming hunter. He bent in front of me and linked his hands together to form a step. I gripped Thomas's reins at the neck, stuck my left knee in the man's hands and heaved up to sit astride Thomas. Thomas stood still, probably thinking about dinner. Or his bowels.

'Right. So, er, shall we?' I looked across to Mindy, who sat slightly lower than me on her hunter, looking neat and trim in her hacking jacket and blue riding hat. My riding hat was too tight and I had forced it up to sit on top of my bonce, releasing the pressure it otherwise exerted on my brow. This looked ridiculous, but saved me from looking and feeling as if someone had fitted a ratchet strap round my head when I took it off. I didn't have a hacking jacket as such, but was wearing a farmer's tweed jacket bought from our local farm store, Countrywide, for the simple reason that it cost roughly one-third the price of a proper hacking jacket and was, to all intents and purposes, exactly the same. Apart from the cut across the shoulders, where mine sagged and bagged a bit. And the pockets, which bulged out on my hips where I had stuffed Mindy's car keys. And the cloth, which, while resembling tweed, was something closer to sandpaper to the touch and regularly reduced the soft flesh around my neck to a pulverised, red, lumpy mess if it got the chance to chafe at it for three or four seconds.

'Where are we actually going then?' I pulled the jacket collar away from my neck and looked around, shading my eyes from the low, watery sun with a gloved hand. Still hoping for, though not entirely succeeding in achieving, the heroic, manly look.

'Well, the school might be the best place to start. Put him through his paces a bit. See what he can do. Hey, old boy, show him what you're up to,' and the pleasant horsey chap slapped Thomas's neck playfully. Thomas chewed at the bit, probably wondering what interesting effects it might produce at the other end if he managed to ingest it. I felt a wobble of nerves and potential embarrassment at the phrase 'put him through his paces'. I'm not an especially great horseman. As was demonstrated when we made a *Top Gear* film recreating the banned pastime of foxhunting by substituting Jeremy in a small 4x4 Suzuki for the fox. In the meeting when it first came up, we all agreed without hesitation that any sensitivities on the part of the public concerning the pursuit of poor foxy-woxy by what the media at large still insists on portraying as a bunch of chinless toffs drenched in bloodlust would be allayed by the prospect of replacing the fox – a cunning, self-serving predator with a nose for trouble and a habit of killing for fun – with Jeremy Clarkson – roughly the same sort of thing as the fox really, only bigger; with worse hair.

And so a plan was devised. It would be, we figured, in essence, a routine test of a new off-roader from a popular manufacturer. This was real-world consumer information of just the type from which the BBC has forged its international reputation as a solid, dependable and sensible broadcaster of quality, considered programming. So, with the car painted up as the fox, complete with brush, Jeremy would set off across the fields, laying a scent trail for the hounds, and the hunt would pursue him on horseback. This would give us, as journalists and car experts, the chance to assess the new off-roader's abilities off the road, across fields and, critically, while being pursued by many dogs. Useful stuff to today's consumer, no doubt.

Of course, it called for someone from the team to ride a horse with the hunt, to show the other side of the story. That job, inevitably, fell to me. The thing is, I may have exaggerated a little when I had spoken in the past about my horse-riding ability. In so much as I may possibly have led other members of the team to believe that I could. Ride, that is. My approach to equestrianism tends to be not so much one where horse and rider bond wordlessly and enjoy a seamless and constant flow of sophisticated communication, opening a channel through which they can both express themselves physically and, perhaps, spiritually in pursuit of a chosen and mutually desired goal in a balletic scene that elevates the essential utilitarianism of the bond 'twixt man and beast to a plane perhaps best described as art – I just try hard not to fall off.

In fact, at the time the *Top Gear* team rather called my bluff by inviting me to ride with the Ledbury Hunt on television in the course of making our film, I had never fallen off. It had looked pretty bloody likely on occasion, and I'm really not certain I could ever explain quite how I hadn't fallen off following some of my clumsier and less elegant bouts of arm flailing, boot waving horseback panic, but, nevertheless, I have always stayed on and have what is termed, I believe, in proper hunting circles 'a good seat'. Indeed, in coarser, less proper horse-riding circles, the same quality is given the epithet 'a sticky bum'; but given that I suspect the same phrase is used rather more often and for quite different reasons in veterinary and nursery nurse circles, I've always stuck with 'a good seat'.

Called upon to apply my excellent seat to a borrowed horse and charge across the fields of my home county, flanked by friends and neighbours resplendent in hunting pinks in pursuit of Jeremy in a 4x4, I performed the sort of jump at the opportunity that I could certainly never have managed on horseback. In fact, jumping was a bit of an issue. I may have sort of given the general, vague impression that I could jump on a horse. Well, specifically, that I could leap atop the most frothy-mouthed of dangerous chargers and hurl it, even against its will, at towering obstacles and clear them effortlessly and per-

172

fectly. Possibly while wearing a big, baggy shirt and shouting 'hah!' at the top of my voice and brandishing a cavalry sword. Like I said, I may have exaggerated a little in the past when discussing my horseback escapades with the team on Monday mornings following weekends when I had, in reality, wobbled around a field on a fat cob, but somehow the event, in the telling, became rather more dynamic and exciting. And now I was in the poo a little bit because, if I were to ride with the hunt, I would have to join them as they leapt fences and hedges in fearless and bold pursuit of the fox, namely Jezza in his 4x4. Awkward, really.

I quietly booked a few riding lessons with heroic local horsewoman Tor Brewer. At her riding school just down the road from my home in Gloucestershire, she put me atop one of her own horses and soon had me effortlessly clearing poles literally several inches off the ground. The hedges and fences on the hunt would probably be several feet higher and can rise to be six feet high and six feet deep. So I still had some work to do and would probably have to choose carefully which obstacles I decided to have a go at on the day and when I had to allow caution to take the reins and slip round the corner through the gate instead.

The day came and a horse was delivered to the field for me to ride. The hunt met, joined this time by our TV crew, at a farm on an appropriately damp, chilly morning. The fields lay muddy and, to my eyes at least, sinister, on all sides, bordered by lethal hedges and fences over which I would shortly be trying to jump the horse that the production team had, with Mindy's help, arranged for me to borrow. It was called Harry and he looked like a collapsed tent; a really big collapsed tent. After some initial difficulty getting on board, things got worse. The hunt traditionally gathers in one place and sort of stands around, its members mounted on their horses, talking about the day, the weather, their hopes for the ride to come and their feelings about their steed. On this particular morning, they may have found this relaxing and comforting element of their hunting ritual slightly harder to enjoy, with Harry and me blundering about among them. There was something wrong with his handbrake. Every other horse stood patiently, flanks gleaming, nostrils flaring, withers, er, withering, its tack shining and its rider perched on top, taking big swigs from the stirrup cup and chatting with a neighbour about previous escapades in the field. Harry refused to stand still and shifted about constantly, taking a few steps to the left, crashing into a big chestnut hunter carrying a man with a moustache. I apologised sheepishly, waved a glove at the moustache and Harry set off backwards, ramming his big arse into the face of the horse behind, whose lady rider spilled sloe gin on her crisp, white stock shirt and laughed in a way that suggested she might be laughing simply because the only alternative was to beat me to death with a riding crop, which would be making a bit too much of a scene this early in the morning.

'Sorry. No brakes. Y'see. Er ...' Harry took off again, blundering to the right, rammed his broad flanks and my right leg deep into the belly of a sturdy old carthorse of a thing to my right, whose rider, a very pleasant Welsh chap, laughed, tipped his glass in my direction and toasted our success in the day to come. Just as this was becoming as intolerable for me as it was for the rest of the hunt, and I teetered on the brink of hopping off Harry's sagging back and seeing if I couldn't knock the bugger to the ground with a punch, there was a commotion from beyond the holding pen. A horn sounded and the hounds 'gave voice'. 'Gave voice' is the official hunting term for what you or I would call 'barking'. If you should ever find yourself joining a hunt for the day – and I suggest you do if you possibly can, they are the loveliest people, down-to-earth, tough and welcoming without exception – do not be tempted to call it barking. You'll receive a hard stare if you do. Neither should you ever, ever, under any circumstances whatsoever refer to the hounds as dogs. I did it once and when I close my eyes now I can still see the looks I got. They are *hounds*. And let that be an end to it. Nevertheless, the hounds of the Ledbury were giving voice to signal that Jeremy, as the fox, had set off across the field, dragging a cloth doused in fox scent for the hounds to follow. After an agreed five-minute wait, the whipper-in bloke who looks after the dogs – God, sorry, hounds – sounded the horn to signal the first draw and, well, there are a lot of terms for what we did which was, basically, set off.

We crossed a short, sloping field of dark green grass and arrived at the first fence, which looked to me to be about twenty feet high but which was, in reality, closer to three, possibly four feet. The rest of the field gave various stirring shouts, kicked their horses on and cleared it in a shower of mud, grass, bravery and gin. Each one, man or woman, young or old, sailed over the fence and landed in the rough field beyond, looking heroic, brave and exciting enough to be worthy of a painting. I sort of sidled up to the fence on Harry and inspected it, resisting the temptation to actually sniff it as a dog might a new piece of furniture at home but leaned down from the saddle and ran a finger across the damp, rough-grained wood. I sat up and drew Harry back a good hundred yards or so across the field. I felt a run-up might be appropriate and, as the rest of the riders had long since charged off through the woods ahead in a flurry of horn blasts and shouting hounds, no one could actually witness my rather more cautious approach to my first ever jump.

I kicked Harry in the ribs, apologised for doing so, did so again and we set off towards the wooden stock fence at a kind of lumbering canter. In fact, the horse, commonly, has four gaits available to the rider. The first and slowest is the Walk. This is a steady gait that is exactly what its name suggests: the horse walks and this is the gait most commonly used for warming the animal up before more strenuous exercise begins. The second gait is the Trot; this is, essentially, a more vigorous walk but, dynamically, an entirely different experience for both horse and rider. More effort is required from the rider to keep the horse 'up together' in the Trot and often he or she must rise and fall smartly in the saddle with the rhythm of the Trot, both to remain comfortable and signal to the horse to stay at this pace. The third gait, the Canter, is possibly the most effective in covering ground; a gentle run, it is used on the approach to jumps and offers the best compromise between endurance and speed. The final, fourth 'gear' is the Gallop, which is basically a full-tilt run as fast as the horse can go. This cannot realistically be maintained for long, although racehorses will specialise in maintaining the gallop for longer and longer periods.

Interestingly, the Icelandic pony adds a fifth gait to this list, the Tolt. Somewhere between a Trot and a Canter, it's surprisingly fast and can be maintained for long stretches at a time. Harry and I, though, introduced an entirely new gait that day, the Slump. A sort of lumpen, arrhythmic stagger, it's not fast and it neither looks nor feels good, is ungainly, ill balanced and can be maintained for only a few minutes before the horse, necessarily a pretty tired old knacker to have attempted the Slump in the first place, keels over dead with the effort of loping along slightly faster than a snail but significantly slower than a small dog, or the rider simply throws himself to the ground with the misery, shame and boredom of it all.

As we Slumped closer to the target, I pointed Harry slap-bang at the middle of the fence, closed my eyes and tried to remember to lean forward in the saddle. Or should it be backwards? Bloody hell; forgotten. I felt the ground leave beneath us as Harry launched himself at the fence. He must have jumped it, because when I opened my eyes there was no fence in front of us; it was receding behind. And up ahead were the woods where the rest of the huntsmen and women had galloped moments earlier.

I hear their shouts and the hounds further ahead in the distance. I was over the fence, my first fence. And I had cleared it.

And now I was totally and hopelessly lost. Fortunately, my tutor's sister, had volunteered – or been volunteered – to look after me on the day of the hunt and had waited behind by the first few trees on the edge of the woods. This meant that, sadly for my ego, she had seen my approach to the fence and had probably been able to make out, even at this distance, that my eyes were firmly shut, but it also meant that we could rely on her more experienced and able senses to find the rest of the field and reunite us with, not only my fellow riders, but also the film crew there to turn the experience into something the viewing public might choose to enjoy on a Sunday evening. Glancing back at the low-lying, sagging fence I had just jumped, I reflected that perhaps this was another film out of which I could not really hope to emerge covered in glory.

I kicked Harry on, hoping for a springing canter to follow my minder on her sprightly mount on the narrow paths through the woods. Harry responded by breaking into a reluctant and lumpy trot and farting at every third step until I caught up in a cloud of gas and raucous noise. What the hell is it with horses?

'Bit windy, is he?'

'Yes. Erm, diet.' I felt myself blush, grateful at least that Harry had shouldered the blame without my having to attribute the outburst to him and risk appearing as protesting too much. My minder looked rather good in her hunting outfit – huntswomen generally do – and slumping up to her aboard a grinning gas bag, heralded by a bout of equestrian flatulence capable of downing an entire field of cane was hardly the sort of James Bond approach I would have wanted in the situation.

'Right, then, let's find the rest, shall we? Er, which way'd they go? I didn't see. Sorry,' I blustered and wished Mindy had been able to ride with me to look after the complicated stuff. But she had the girls to look after and was waiting back at the farm, no doubt keen to hear my stories of derring-do and bravery on board my mighty charger. When I eventually did return, muddy, bruised and embarrassed after a day during which I never quite mastered the art of riding over jumps, riding on the flat, riding up or down hills, sitting still, mounting or dismounting, I made some up for her – strictly out of a desire to spare her disappointment. I am a selfless kind of guy like that.

*

The sand school was flanked by elderly wood-built stables and barns and bordered, as is traditional, by half-round wooden-rail fencing. The wood was bleached with age and blended with the biscuit colour of the soft sand beneath it to create a gentle, country scene fit for a biscuit tin lid.

'Well, if they don't move their fat arses out of the way, how can I get into the school at all,' I hissed at Mindy as she waited patiently at the gate to the school, hands resting at the pommel, reins draped casually between them. We were waiting for two ladies on horseback to clear the gate so that we could walk in and begin in earnest my road test of Thomas. If he worked out okay, I would borrow him the following day for a romantic ride out with Mindy. We might even take a picnic and tie the horses up by an idyllic stream for an hour or two.

The sturdy ladies cleared the sand school and the gate lay open in front of us. Mindy kicked on in front of me and I tapped Thomas with my heels, urging him through the gate and on to the welcoming sand beyond. Maybe he didn't fancy it; maybe he was troubled by some further complication of his unfathomably busy intestinal system. Or maybe he just didn't like me. Whatever the cause, the ensuing accident was prefaced and, indeed, signalled by him looking up quickly; there was no sudden noise to startle him, no barking dog, backfiring car or squealing child. I could see or hear nothing that might startle a horse at home, in its own familiar surroundings. The tree in the field to our right merely stood there, being a tree, as it had always been. The fence carried on with being a fence and the barn concentrated all of its effort on being a barn and remaining perfectly still. But something flicked the switch labelled 'panic' in Thomas's head. And panic he did, beginning the process with a large and really quite impressively athletic jump to the left. If you're of a similar age to me, the phrase 'jump to the left' will be followed immediately by 'step to the right' together with recollections of the outrageously camp antics of *The Rocky Horror Show* in the eighties. But that was the problem; there was no 'step to the right'. Had there been, I might have regained my balance. Instead, Thomas carried on with his jump to the left and I lurched to the right and began the business of falling off.

It wasn't a fast fall; far from it, in fact. I had time to look across to see Mindy's horse twenty feet away from mine as she turned into the centre of the sand school and looked back to take in my predicament. Good; she would see me fall off and consider me brave and heroic. Hoorah – so, back on with the business of falling off then. It gradually became obvious that I was shortly to be parting company entirely with Thomas's sagging back and I figured some sort of roll might be the best option.

I tucked my right shoulder in as I rolled forwards and passed his neck, my until now 'good seat' leaving the saddle with ease, showing not a trace of its much praised sticky-ness to keep it in place. I rolled a bit more, my shoulder now tucking further under, and I felt it likely that I would land on my back. Not bad news, really; it was called a sand school for good reason, after all, the soft surface providing a welcome landing for unfortunate riders like me who came unstuck. And just as I really felt I might actually become bored by the process of this fall unfolding with almost unnatural slowness, the ground arrived. It always does and I was in no way surprised by this development, having foreseen its inevitability right from the start of the event. However, there was an issue that suddenly arose and proved itself to be of a most pressing and urgent nature.

On pulling into the yard and parking earlier, I had

stuck the keys to Mindy's Land Rover in the pocket of my not-quite-a-hacking-jacket. This would not perhaps have been such a big deal had life carried on in the way anticipated at the time. But this fall cast rather a different light on the presence of the keys in my jacket pocket. Namely, that they might just grind my pelvis to dust and cripple me for life. Mindy's Land Rover keys were already, even without their soon-to-be-pivotal role in crippling me, something of a bone of contention between us. Partly, this was because of the unnecessarily gaudy nature of the assembly of plastic toys, torches, hoof-scraping implements and keys to houses and cars no longer owned by us that Mindy keeps together with the keys to her Land Rover. But my objections to Mindy's Land Rover keys are not limited purely to the aesthetic – it is the size of the bunch that causes particular offence and that would be of special relevance to me and my pelvis in the next few hundredths of a second.

The whole assembly – toys, keys, torches and all – is kept together, attached to an enormous metal carabiner of the type favoured by rock climbers. These large clasps are made of finely tooled metal and designed to be strong enough to carry the weight of a fully grown and well-developed man suspended over a yawning chasm or a precipice in some desperate rock-climbing situation where life itself depends on the quality of just such a crucial piece of kit. Its importance is of a less critical nature when all it is being called upon to do is corral a bunch of keys, a plastic sheep, a small metal torch that came free with a tank of diesel, a spike for pulling stones out of horses' hooves and a plastic monkey with glowing eyes that cheeps when you press it. However, the hitherto rather drab and unimportant existence of this particular carabiner was enlivened quite suddenly and assumed a rather more physical and critical role, perhaps closer to the level of importance for which it was created, though ultimately of a less positive and benign nature.

It not being an especially well-fitted garment, such as, say, a proper hacking jacket might be, my cheap farmer's not-quite-a-hacking-jacket twisted as I fell, placing the huge bulk of Mindy's Land Rover keys against the base of my spine, just where it joins the pelvis. As the ground arrived, I had settled back, anticipating a not at all unpleasant landing on to the soft sand prior to dusting myself off, sighing to Mindy that it was nothing at all and enjoying my elevated status as a stuntman. They do say that you're not really a proper rider until you've fallen off and I was quietly glad to be getting my first fall out of the way in a controlled situation, on a soft surface and, best of all, with Mindy to witness it. However, as my back touched down, the sinister presence of her Land Rover keys became immediately apparent when they made an attempt to bolt for freedom via my spine, pelvis and intestines.

Lying there now, staring up at the pale blue sky, I knew that something was wrong, but still had not quite worked out what.

'Erm, don't call an ambulance, nothing broken or anything, don't worry, but I don't think I can actually sort of get up.' Mindy dismounted and ran over to where I lay.

As she arrived I sat up, glad that things were working well enough to allow that, but still confused by signals racing back from the pelvis department to tell me that all was not well. I tried bending my legs to hook my feet under me, ready to stand; surprisingly, it worked. I flexed my left leg, accepted Mindy's extended hand and gingerly stood. I placed weight on to my right leg. It worked too and I walked slowly over to the fence bordering the school. Something was still wrong, though; more messages were arriving, all in a terrible panic, from the base of my spine and my pelvis. I reached the fence and lifted my right leg up on to the lower rail, feeling strangely compelled to stretch it out as I might before a run. When I put it back to the ground I found the leg less willing to accept any weight. And then less still until it flatly refused to bear anything at all. I leaned on the rail.

'I'm stuck. Sorry. Leg's buggered. Dunno what it is, but bring the Land Rover over, please, and let's get off to hospital 'cos something's wrong. Not broken a bone, feels like a nerve or something.'

Mindy paused for a second before asking for her keys. I fished them out of my pocket and handed her the huge, bulky assembly, already guessing that there would be a dent almost perfectly replicating its complex shape somewhere on my lower back. Mindy weighed the keys in her hand, her mouth dropping open slightly.

'Were they in your pocket when you …?' She looked back at the dent in the ground where I had landed just moments before.

'Yup. Think that's what did it. Whatever it is I've done.'

I winced as more strange signals from my jangled nerves raced around my system. A lorry passed on the road beyond the sand school. I thought of Gloucester hospital, some twenty miles away, and I hoped that I hadn't damaged anything seriously.

'Oh, bloody hell. You never ride with keys in your …' Mindy thought better of finishing the obvious statement and I saw immediately, and from very personal experience, the wisdom of such a policy among more experienced horse riders.

After some good-natured joshing concerning my inability to stay away from hospitals, during which I smiled regally and ground my teeth to powder, the nurses at Gloucester hospital pronounced my leg to be unbroken and the source of my growing discomfort and complete inability to place any weight on my right leg was determined as a flexed sacroiliac joint. This cartilaginous joint in the pelvis is a very common place for horse riders to hurt themselves and feels much akin to slipping a disc in the spine. Mine was not broken or burst or split or any of the other dramatic descriptions I had secretly hoped might be attributed to it, but was, instead, just strained. This was the equivalent, I decided, of being told by the doctor that the stomachache you had rather hoped might earn you a day off school was probably down to nerves or overeating, if anything at all, and there was more than likely nothing wrong. I sat up on the hospital bed on which I had been wheeled back from the X-ray department and looked down at my knees. Once again, they were draped in the blue and white folds of the flowery nightie that does up at the back. I glanced up to Mindy; she was sitting alongside the bed in a grey plastic chair, still in her riding kit.

'Your jacket stinks of horses,' I pointed out. 'They'll probably throw us out.'

'Yeah, well, I'm not the plonker who rode with keys in his pocket and broke his bottom falling off a horse as a result.'

'I haven't broken my bottom, I've flexed my sacry-whatever joint and it's really quite nasty.' I rotated my foot on the end of the leg in question. 'Actually a very painful injury.' And I leaned forward off the bed to lower myself on to my left leg before gently putting the right to the ground and leaning some weight on to it. I shrieked, a girly, high-pitched yelp, and saw stars. It really did hurt now, like a bugger and I understood that the crutches the nurse had brought in and propped up against the bedside cabinet really would be necessary as more than badges to prove my injury.

'Bloody hellfire, that hurts like hell. Where's the car?'

Mindy stood and explained that she had ended up parking it some distance away while the nurses checked out my broken bottom, but she would go and get it and pick me up opposite the ambulance arrival point down the corridor. The porter would wheel me out there in a chair or, if I preferred, I could always walk.

No, I did not prefer to walk, thanks, not when someone let off a Taser gun in my hip if I placed more than a milligram of weight on it, I didn't.

✳

'Yes, but surely they'll be suspicious. I mean, look at it.'

Leaning against the bedroom wall, I turned the metal crutch over in my hands, inspecting it closely as I spoke to Mindy on the other side of the room, across a mountain of clothes and kit as I packed for a month-long trip around the world. 'It could have anything concealed in it. Drugs, a knife, the whole thing could be an elaborately disguised gun of some sort.' I lofted the crutch on to my shoulder and squinted down its length.

'Darling, this is not the first time someone with a poorly leg, or a broken bottom, has tried to get on an aeroplane, so they will have thought of it.' Mindy sighed as she spoke. 'Anyway, you can't walk without them, so what choice have you got? At worst, they'll take the crutches separately and put you in a wheelchair.'

I shuddered at the thought. It would look too much like I was trying to attract attention to myself. 'Look at *me*, I'm off the telly and I've hurt my leg. Look!' A couple of years earlier, asked by an airline if we wanted assistance at the other end, Mindy and I had preened ourselves at our new-found celebrity status and said that, yes, that would be smashing, thanks, as we had the girls with us. And so, on landing, we were met at the door of the aeroplane by a uniformed member of the ground crew and, for me anyway, a dull sense of foreboding. At the end of the ramp, the airline operative indicated an enormous electric cart with a blue canvas roof and grinned a slightly knowing grin.

'Your chariot.' He bowed and waved a hand at the cart as he spoke, in a thick accent, the only two words he uttered during the ordeal through which he then put us. The girls were delighted, squealing with excitement as they climbed on to the cart's broad bench seats. Mindy looked less happy as she followed them like someone mounting the gallows. She, too, had worked it out. I took up the rear-facing bench at the back of the machine, alone and dumbstruck by the horror of what I now realised was about to happen. Our driver grinned again, threw one hand in the hair and, with the other, must have hit a button or turned a key, causing two things to happen simultaneously: the chariot moved forward very slowly and began an insistent and very loud beeping as it inched across the carpet of the arrivals terminal.

I tried to stare only at the floor; to ignore the people around us. I focused on the repetitive, geometric pattern of the blue carpet as it passed slowly beneath our wheels. Izzy and Willow twisted on their seats, asked if this was as fast as it could go and shouted over the beeping to Mindy that they were loving it and that this was the best bit of the holiday.

'Look, Hippo thinks it's great.' Izzy held up her bright pink stuffed hippo toy, a favourite of hers and a regular traveller on our holidays. Mindy sat still, her hands in her lap and her eyes fixed on the girls. And all the time, as I stared at the carpet, I knew that people were looking at us, wondering who I thought I was that I felt it necessary to have my family specially transported across the airport terminal in a machine that emitted a constant and irri-

tating beep just to make sure no one missed what I, presumably, must consider the edifying spectacle of me with
my wife and two daughters, all of us pale-faced and red-
eyed from an overnight, long-haul flight, sitting on plastic
cushions and cheating the passport queue. Once again, I
found myself longing for death to step up behind me,
clear its skeletal throat and cleave my head from my miserable body. And so, no, I wouldn't be calling upon the
airline staff to wheel me to the aircraft today; I would
stagger my way there on bleeding stumps of shattered
bone first.

Exactly one week after learning that Thomas probably
wasn't the horse for me, I met up with the crew at
Heathrow, ready for the first flight on the first leg of our
World Tour. Although legs were, of course, a slightly
touchy subject with me at that point – I was on crutches.
I had taken the precaution of phoning Chris's office to let
them know that I might be doing the first few shows
with slightly fewer legs than I had traditionally brought
to the party. I figured it better to let him and his team
digest the news in their own time rather than present
them with it at the airport on the day of departure. As it
was, it just meant that I had given them more time to
prepare their piss-taking efforts. Chris bounded up to me
in the departure lounge, pointed to his own, fully functioning complement of legs, grinned and asked by how
much I would be dropping my fee as it seemed that half
of what I had brought with me wasn't working.

'Bugger off, Chris, it hurts like a bastard, but don't
worry, I'll be able to do everything I did at the shows in

London and Dublin.' Chris smiled again and we got on with the business of catching up, sharing news and settling in for what was going to be a very, very long trip indeed. We were taking the same show that we had just finished performing in London, Birmingham and Dublin around the world; first to South Africa, then on to Sydney, New Zealand and Hong Kong. But secretly, since, as Mindy still insisted on referring to it, 'breaking my bottom', I had wondered just how I was going to do the show. In one sequence, we had been performing a low-rent tribute to Evel Knievel It called for me to ride out in a ridiculous fat-suit and perform a tribute jump to my hero, the greatest daredevil of them all, Mr E. Knievel. It was very funny and not remotely dangerous – the motorcycle was one of those tiny ones for kids, the ramp I used was only about a foot high and the bus over, or rather through, which I jumped was a balsa replica – but it was a jump nonetheless, which meant it involved, as well as a take-off, a landing. I really couldn't see how my one good leg could possibly support me on landing, even from a couple of feet in the air, and I knew that it would still be a few weeks before my right leg could bear weight. I mulled it over as I hobbled down the ramp to the plane – I had turned down the inevitable offer of a wheelchair from the check-in woman with a shudder and a wince she must have thought most confusing and unnecessary – and settled down for the overnight flight to Johannesburg.

There is, I discovered, a technique to performing a low-rent, comedy motorcycle jump with a bad hip joint following a low-speed fall off a horse on to your wife's Land Rover keys that wrenched your sacry-whatever joint because you were too mean to pay for a properly fitting hacking jacket. And that technique specifically involves ensuring you remain at the legal and medical limit of your intake of powerful painkillers at all times when performing the show. And as we were performing the show two, three or four times every day, this meant very much, at all times. It worked, though; the landings were softened by the bike's soft, long travel suspension anyway and, with a few simple grunts and gasps, the whole process amounted to no more than a brief burst of pain through my hip and a looming sense of dread as the moment approached at which I would appear onstage in my comedy fat-suit and berate the show's producers for fitting it with too much padding while the audience – usually – laughed at the ridiculous spectacle of a man suddenly as wide as he was tall. Then I would hobble off-stage again to collect the bike, leaving Jeremy and Sasha to laugh with the audience at the diminutive scale of the jump I had assembled in the arena and switch the tiny, one-foot-tall model buses I had placed at the end of the ramp with a much larger one as a 'surprise' for me when I rode back onstage ready for my Evel Knievel tribute leap. As an extra touch, they set fire to the arch at the end of the ramp, claiming it was in an attempt to make it more visible for me for 'Health and Safety' reasons. It was a fun sketch and, apart from seeing stars on every landing, it worked well.

The South African shows were fun to do. The audience

knows us well over there and seems to get what the stage show is about. But it didn't feel, to us, like we were on a world tour yet. For us to feel that we would have to go somewhere we hadn't yet been. And that was about to happen as we took the whole effort – crew, scenery, cars, the lot – to Sydney.

＊

I'm very glad that I'm able to say 'wow' at stuff, to be overwhelmed or overawed – because, as a Brummie, I probably shouldn't be. It's a Birmingham thing: put a Brummie anywhere, in front of the most astonishing spectacle in the world, but don't expect him to stand open-mouthed and impressed. The biggest reaction you'll get will be some observation to the effect that their mate had one a bit like it once/has already been there/didn't like the food or knew the owner and thought him a bit of a wally. Don't ask me why; it's not as though our hometown is punctuated by stark and beautiful evidence of lost civilisations and natural wonders. I've been to Sparkhill, Hall Green, Moseley and Knowle and none of them is the Hanging Gardens of Babylon. But whatever the romantic, architectural, artistic and historical qualifi-cations of our city, we're not an easily impressed bunch. I am bloody easily impressed, though. I look up at stuff and say 'wow' on pretty much an hourly basis. And I was doing it again now.

'Bloody hell.' I craned my neck to look around the arena. It stood five balconies high, the seats extending up into the gloom far, far overhead. 'Well, it's certainly big enough. And we're really going to fill this?' I spoke to no one in particular; the rest of the team was wandering around the arena floor having roughly similar experiences. At least, all those who, like me, had not yet visited the Acer Arena at the Sydney Olympic Park, the largest indoor live entertainment and sporting arena in Australia, where we were to stage our show. This was part of the complex built in 1999 to host the 2000 Olympic Games and the advance publicity proudly proclaimed it had used enough concrete in building it to fill eight-and-a-half Olympic swimming pools, was the size of eight rugby union pitches and could house an audience of 21,000 people. The idea that our ridiculous car show could possibly warrant a 21,000-seat stadium was more than a little ridiculous. We wandered about as a group, moving from one area to another and getting a feel for the place. In the front hall, stands had been erected housing supercars and attractions for the throngs of visitors that would, we had been assured, be travelling hundreds of miles across Australia.

'Well, it really is all ours to balls up now, then,' I muttered to myself as I approached the glass doors that let out on to the sun-bleached concourse in front of the arena. Beyond, in the brilliant light of what was to be one of the hottest days anywhere on earth, I saw Jeremy. He was marching about the pavement, looking up at the front of the arena overhead, his camera in hand and a strange look on his face. I slipped outside and joined him and he pointed back to the building. On the vast frontage, three huge posters stood side by side. On one, it proclaimed that Coldplay were coming on their 'Viva La Vida' tour, and there, in the middle, directly over the doors, was another and it said simply 'For the First Time in Australia Top Gear Live' and featured pictures of me and Jeremy.

'Shit. Never thought I'd see that in my lifetime.'

Jeremy lowered his camera and grinned. We were really on a world tour now. The schedule called for us to rehearse through the afternoon and the following morning and then to be ready for the first show that night. And we were already looking forward to it.

Back at the hotel, we discovered just one slight problem with our newly invigorated world tour. We didn't have a show: at least none of the stage equipment, props, cars, stunt equipment or scenery. We had used a duplicate set for South Africa, and loaded the original kit from our shows in the UK on to a cargo ship bound for Australia long before we left. It should have arrived in Sydney harbour two weeks earlier. But it hadn't. This had been common knowledge for a week or so now, but Chris and his team had chosen to keep it from those of us not directly involved with such matters, figuring that it would only wind us up and, anyway, what could we possibly do about it other than worry needlessly? And they were right, of course. I had slept soundly on the plane over from South Africa and enjoyed an excellent night out on landing. This might not have been so easy had I been aware that we were about to face the show-business equivalent of doing school PE in your pants because you've forgotten your gym kit. As it was, Chris and his senior officers, James, Baz and Gemma, looked pretty stressed as they sat in earnest conversation at a table in the hotel's quiet bar. Hardly surprising, really; I don't imagine Chris or any of them were looking forward to explaining to the 70,000 Australians who had already bought tickets that the show wasn't quite as advertised on the posters and would actually consist of Jeremy and me on an empty stage telling knock-knock jokes and challenging each other to a do-nut competition in stolen airport luggage trolleys.

There was a brief break in the clouds. The problem was not quite as bad as it had, at first, seemed. The ship containing everything we needed to avoid a dose of shame and embarrassment larger than had ever been witnessed or conceived in global history was, in fact, in Australia but caught up in the docks behind another container ship, which couldn't be moved right now. I guess the dockers were doing the maritime version of asking over the Tannoy in a bar if the owner of the blue Astra parked in front of the bins could move it so the beer lorry could get past. So this wasn't the end of the world, I ventured. I mean, surely someone with the keys to the other boat will turn up, they can haul it out of the road and get ours on to the platform, or whatever, to unload it. Nobody smiled as I spoke and it was explained to me, quite crisply I thought, that there was a further complication: everything in the ship had to be checked by customs and then processed through a decontamination operation because Australia is very careful about such things and a boatload of what must look to normal eyes like a load of old scrap, recently imported from Ye Olde Englande, would doubt-less be considered a potential breeding ground for disease and germs virulent enough to render the continent life-less and empty. Essentially, then, we were still doomed to die on a space station, but the supply ship bringing oxygen and food was moored up on the moon and we could wave at them while we starved and choked to death. Nice. The stress levels in the room rose still further and I felt it prudent to keep such quips and observations to myself lest a member of the production team felt com-pelled to kick my teeth out through the back of my neck as a means of loosening up a bit and clearing his head.

In the end a mission was decided upon. Chris, as a hands-on kind of bloke, would travel down to the docks himself. He would take with him two members of his team: Baz Bungish had already been in Australia for a week as an advance party, paving the way to getting the problem solved. He would go with Chris and they would take as their ambassadorial and diplomatic representative James Cooke-Priest, the Brand Events commercial director and the world's most polite and patient man, who would doubtless be useful should Chris or Baz find themselves close to losing their temper with some oily-pawed, grizzle-chinned Aussie docker with the keys to their toy box on his belt.

And they set off, simple as that. We sat in open-mouthed awe, inspired by their bravery and selfless sacrifice.

'They'll all be killed,' Jeremy proffered.

'Almost certainly,' I nodded in solemn agreement.

'Shit.'

'Yeah. Shit.'

We looked around the room.

'Beer?'

'Might as well.'

Other members of the team joined Jeremy and me in the bar as we awaited the return of Chris, Baz and James from the frontline. Together, we tried our hardest not to worry too much about their fate by bolstering our spirits with friendly, comforting talk and equally comforting cool beer. We had grown quite comforted by the time the heroes of the raid on Botany Bay returned to HQ in the bar, but we tried our best to give them a stirring welcome appropriate to their recent exploits. Indeed, we may even have sung a song or two and suggested the casting of a special medal. Over a few more beers – actually, a great many more – we went over and over the details of their daring mission and the very real possibility that it might turn out to have saved the day for us all. The ship blocking the dockers' access to our own had been moved – maybe the bloke came back from the bogs, twirling the keys on his fingers, entirely unaware of the stress he had caused, but it was gone and that was the main thing. That left the business of decontamination of the contents. Heated and intense negotiations between Chris and the Australian officer in charge of proceedings had resulted – not, as I proffered, in a rare case of deportation back from Australia to London for Chris – in the securing of an agreement whereby the decontamination could be limited to just a few pieces of kit. Principally, and this is where you can't help but agree with them, the Australian decontamination operatives – and there's a business card you really don't want to be carrying – were interested in the item of equipment used in a feature we had named 'the Colander of Death'. Not the snappiest title, I agree, but it's a great stunt, consisting of an enormous metal cage, spherical in shape and made of thin strips of metal so that it forms something like a giant tea-bag strainer, or, indeed, a colander, and inside which motorcyclists can ride around. It works rather like the famous old wall of death routines, but it is a sphere and so affords the riders the scope to pilot their bikes in pretty much any direction through all 360 degrees.

Better still, as part of the act and as a punishment for some misdemeanour or other I had committed earlier in each show – the exact nature of which tended to vary from show to show and could be something as serious as messing up a driving sequence or just having silly hair – I was forced to stand in the cage while the bikes rode around it. Tremendous; there's a spectacle, the glamour of the bikes and the remote possibility that I could be killed at any moment, ground to a pulp and forced out of the holes in the cage like lamb through a mincer: everyone wins. One tiny thing though, it's French. The riders, the organisers of the stunt and the kit itself were all French and the Australians took a dim view of this. And although you can kind of see their point here, it was not, it must be said, the most diplomatic piece of international relationship-fostering, when the Aussies insisted on taking the entire sphere out of the ship's hold and decontaminating it before allowing it into the country. No doubt they would, had they been allowed, have gone on to insist on steam-cleaning and disinfecting the Frenchmen themselves, naked on the dockside, but we drew the line at that. It would have been funny though. Under the terms of the now famous international treaty drawn up, ratified and agreed in record time following the daring raid on Botany Bay by Chris and his soldiers, the Colander of Death would be processed through decontamination sharpish and delivered to us ready to rehearse the show the following day. The Frenchmen were free to roam as they chose, even to shake hands with people. We had a show. And it was highly likely that we would also all have hangovers the following day.

✳

The first show went well, though not without the odd complication. I may, in fact, have made a bit of a knob of myself immediately before we went onstage to face a crowd of 7,500 baying Aussies. The earplugs we wear to present these shows, the very earplugs that had, indirectly, triggered Chris's heart attack when they gave me an ear infection that led to me facing him with blood trickling out of my recently damaged head, have been the source of endless entertainment over the years. Obviously, a tiny proportion of the entertainment provided has been that enjoyed by the crowds who have visited the shows in which we wear them. Although, to be quite honest, that enjoyment has been purely incidental and the bulk of it has rather been confined to us. And it's that sense of confinement that lies at the very heart of their ability to entertain.

Once we've jammed them into our ears, we enter our own world. The earplugs themselves are a perfect fit, having been custom-built, as I have said, for the wearer, and so create an excellent seal, cutting out everything from our lugholes but the sounds fed into them directly by the tiny speakers buried in the plugs. And the only sounds to reach them are those picked up by the microphones we carry or wear, Madonna-style, on our cheeks. In other words, we can only hear each other. Musicians use the same system so that they can follow the beat and play their parts accurately in a loud stadium. For them it's an essential tool, allowing them to focus their energies and talents into the creation and honing of their art form for the appreciation of their admiring audience. For us it's so that in a noisy, echoing arena, full of pumping beats and shrieking engines from whatever act we're performing or introducing, we can hear our cue lines and hurl insults at one another for the delight of our – probably bored, but too polite to say it – audience.

We discovered quite early on – well, the very first time we used them, in fact, in London in 2008 – that the earplugs, their associated radio receivers and the microphones don't just work on the stage itself. They work pretty much everywhere in the building. We found this out initially – and, perhaps, inevitably – when one of us went for a last-minute pee before hitting the stage. Back then, the show was called *MPH Live* and Jeremy and I had the delight of being joined by Tiff Needell as third presenter. Tiff and Jeremy have worked together for centuries – a fact only made possible by the quite incredibly advanced age of them both – and so had an immediate rapport on and off the stage.

Standing around backstage at Earl's Court, we were waiting to go on for the first time in a run of shows lasting a week. It's a strange, noisy, busy place, backstage at a show like ours. In the dim light, surrounded by black drapes and supercars, dancers stretch out and get ready to go on and perform while burly stagehands move props around and blokes in inexplicable and inexcusable shorts carry clipboards about and look busy, talking into headsets and frowning a lot. We mostly just take the piss and forget what we're about to go on and do. The music rose to a crescendo in our earplugs and we readied ourselves to drive on in our cars, spin do-nuts, and, hopefully, be greeted by warm cheers. Or a barrage of old fruit and wheel wrenches. Tiff had not yet appeared in the backstage area. He was due to come onstage with us to open the show and I began to wonder if he had wandered off and got lost. Or forgotten what he was doing that day. And then I looked across as quite suddenly the rising throb and wail of our intro music was joined by an altogether different sound – something more organic and natural.

'Bloody hell,' Jeremy lifted his mic to his mouth to shout into it, his voice reaching my earplugs loud and strong over the music and the strange new noise.

'Tiff's taking a piss.'

And he was. A gentle cascade, clearly that of the amber nectar splashing joyfully against the porcelain, rang bell-like through the raucous cacophony assaulting our ears through the earplugs.

'Certainly am, lads. Needed that.' Tiff's voice, echoing around the tiled walls of the gents upstairs, came through loud and clear now. And at that moment an immense panorama of possibilities opened up before all three of us. We realised immediately the significance of this discovery: we had our own world, one not bound by the common rules of sensitivity and censorship, but one to which no invitation could be garnered regardless of status or authority, one to which only those of us about to sally forth together and face the fierce thousands beyond the curtains were admitted. And one in which your mate could take a piss, seemingly right in your ear. Which was most unpleasant.

Within days we had invented new games in our new world. We discovered that it was possible to have a conversation with someone not wearing the same, totally sealed earplugs – so that was anyone who wasn't Tiff, Jeremy or me – only if the earplug-wearer held up his microphone in the face of the non-wearer so that their words passed into the system and thus into the earplugs. This also meant, of course, that the entire conversation was heard by the other two wearers, even if they were standing some way off. Indeed, little else could be heard, as the sound nearest to the microphone of the conversationalist would be, inevitably, his conversation.

Through experimentation and accident, we learned

that it is possible for those not officially part of a conversation to join in, passing handy suggestions for themes and questions to the member of our little team in conversation with an outsider. And, needless to say, some of the suggested questions or topics yelled directly into the ears of whichever of the three of us was attempting to hold a decent and serious conversation quickly became fairly robust and ribald. This was made more awkward by the fact that the non-wearer was never aware of the fact that, all the time they were talking with Tiff or Jeremy or me, we were also listening to a continuous stream of pretty strong comments fed directly into our ears by two people not even in the same room. This, by the way, explains the sometimes puzzling or inappropriate facial expressions we might have pulled while talking with people backstage.

Very quickly – well immediately, in fact – this developed into a game in which one of the three of us would set off and deliberately start a conversation with a stranger while the other two, hiding behind a pillar or a bin, would use their microphones to provide questions for the talker to work into the conversation. These questions were generally not of the 'So, what was the first record you ever bought?' variety, but rather a little stronger and more agricultural in tone. Listening in as the player then set about trying to introduce some of the more challenging questions into a conversation, with a complete stranger not in any way aware that a game was being played, proved a most entertaining way to spend the few minutes backstage before each show began.

Tiff, faced with the challenge of asking an especially delicate question of a largish, middle-aged woman concerning her attitude towards activities reserved, as far as is known, to myth and legend and involving a certain historical female ruler and a beast of burden more commonly used for a very different form of sport than that to which legend claims she put the poor creature, began his line of questioning by asking where she lived. Jeremy and I howled with laughter at his wimpishness and wondered aloud and directly into his burning ears just how the hell he was going to get from there to where we, and we alone, knew he needed to take the conversation. The lady answered that she lived in Guildford. Tiff breezily asked if that was near Lingfield and observed that there was a great deal of equestrian activity in that part of the world. We knew immediately that the game was back on.

It proved a very popular game, at least with us. When James May joined the team in subsequent years and the show became *Top Gear Live*, the game continued with renewed vigour. And now, in Australia, I was back once again in that peculiar, twilight, backstage world of dim lights, strange props and nerves; where the only sounds to reach your ears are those channelled into them through the microphone in your hand and those carried by just two other people. We waited for the signal to step out into the huge, multi-tiered auditorium and do our best to entertain 7,500 people for an hour.

As we stood near our cars, ready to jump in and drive on, various acts readied themselves around us for their part in the show. Some were involved in the sequences going on before we went out there. Others formed part of our introduction, at the climax of which we would hurtle out in supercars, drive around the arena floor pulling huge power slides, stop, get out and introduce our co-host. For the Australian shows we had been joined by one of the presenters from the Australian version of *Top Gear*, a young racing driver called Steve Pizzati, who was standing alone in the gloom by his car and doubtless running through his words in his head, ready for his first night.

Jeremy and I loitered by our cars, ready for the off. Among the performers limbering up around us was a troupe of dancers who would perform a striking musical act involving a supercar and a svelte girl in a skin-tight, red Lycra catsuit carrying a whip. The girl in question was stretching her muscles, the better to be ready to go through her eye-watering routine. Having completed her preparations, she stood around and waited for her cue to go onstage and unleash her warmed-up muscles on the waiting masses.

'Bloody hell, she's amazing.' I spoke into my microphone and tried to catch Jeremy's eyes as my words were fired directly into his ears.

'I mean look …' and then I added some more comments of a reasonably fruity nature concerning the dancer's general fitness, health and ability to fill a skin-tight, red Lycra catsuit. Jeremy looked mildly distracted and didn't respond, so I turned up the wick a little, adding some extra zing to my comments; pointing out, perhaps, the nature and construction of the dancer's thigh boots, pondering the difficulty of finding undergarments offering suitable support to a dancer about to embark on a routine as athletic as that facing the subject of my consideration now. I may or may not have added a great many other increasingly direct and robust comments concerning the nature and construction of the dancer herself. I went on, it must be said, at some considerable length and explored some pretty extreme corners not only of the dancer, her act, her costume and her own various talents, but also of my own imagination. Eventually, after perhaps ten minutes or so, I ground to a halt; my imagination exhausted. I sighed, ran my hand through my hair and added in a final breath,

'I mean, just look at her. She's amazing.'

'Yes, Hammond,' Jeremy spoke for the first time since I had embarked on my unbroken stream of consciousness, 'and she heard every single word of that' he added with a grin. A warm and not at all comfortable feeling swept over and through me.

He stepped back slightly in order to appreciate the whole scene as I began to crumple under the steely gaze of the dancer who suddenly looked not only very sexy, but also very cross. The woman had, of course, heard everything. She didn't need to be privy to our private, closed world, where every comment spoken into or near our microphones was fed directly into our heads through our earplugs, because she was standing two feet away from me and she had been able to hear each and every sordid syllable of my soliloquy by dint of simply listening in, unaided, with her standard-issue ears.

'Oh, Christ man, she did, didn't she?' I looked across at Jeremy and spoke in quick, desperate tones. 'I mean, everything? Even the bit about …' and I repeated one of the more specific of my recent observations. 'Oh, God, she can hear me now, too.' I looked at the dancer, she stared down her nose at me, suddenly haughty, her almond eyes narrowing like a tiger fixing its prey, readying itself for the hunter's lethal sprint. I looked around for escape. There was none. The drapes pressed in around me, I grew hot, and the music onstage rose to a climax. I tried a sheepish grin at the dancer. It didn't seem to help. I wondered if she would kill me quickly or prolong the agony for her own entertainment. And, finally, finally, the show began.

*

'Okay, so does this one count as a helicopter crash?' Technically it did. As Chris frowned with the effort of trying to come up with a pithy answer to my question and with the greater effort, I suspect, of trying not to look scared, the pilot executed a hurried landing back at the Auckland heliport we had left only moments earlier, ready to inspect the damage from what had, beyond all doubt and by any definition, been a helicopter crash. We had all seen it, all been involved and all been very brave in not screaming, offering up frantic prayers or spoiling our best holiday trousers. No one had begged forgiveness before meeting their maker or, worse still, declared a long-standing and deep-seated love for any of their colleagues in order to get it off their chest before crashing into the waiting ocean and dying. In fact, I had missed the actual crash itself, having been busy tackling an especially tricky nasal scab at the time and had just been on the point of asking if anyone else had found that the air conditioning dried up their nostrils as it had mine, when someone announced that we had just had a midair collision and had to land and check for damage. I perked up and asked what had happened and was told that we had hit a seagull only a second or two after taking off. We were on a short pleasure flight, midway through our week in New Zealand and, already, it looked as if it might turn out to be a more exciting flight than anticipated. My question to Chris concerning whether or not this counted as an actual helicopter crash was a valid one, given that we shared a history of getting into difficulty in helicopters on *Top Gear Live.*

✳

Two years earlier, on our second visit to Johannesburg with what was then called *MPH Live*, Chris had offered to take Jeremy and me on a helicopter safari as a thank-you for all of our efforts over the previous few days. We were grateful for the chance to get out and see the sights. And more grateful still for the chance of helping Chris spend some of his money and so accepted his offer eagerly. On the appointed day, a car arrived to drive the three of us out to what we imagined would be an airfield and our waiting chopper. It was one of those African days where the sky remains the gentlest of blues but radiates a heat fierce enough to cook granite. Around us, as we drove out into the bush, the landscape lay rich and green and verdant – a heightened version of what we were used to at home, with richer greens, taller trees, denser undergrowth and much, much bigger vistas.

The car drew up at the entrance to a field of tall, thick grass. And in it we could just see some sort of machine. A few angled panels, a straight line, a flash of white paint gave it away: this was it, our chopper. We hopped out of the car and walked towards a gap in the hedge, feet dragging through the dark, green grass and releasing the scents of the dense undergrowth into the hot air.

A million insects chirruped in the thick foliage around us and I was glad to be in Africa. We were living the dream: a stage show in front of tens of thousands, a chauffeur-driven car – albeit quite an old Toyota – and now a private helicopter to a game reserve and lunch. I sighed with the pleasure of it and memorised the details. And then I snapped out of it pretty sharpish.

'What, uh, the hell is that?' I levelled a finger at the tiny helicopter cowering in the grass ahead of us. Only the top of it appeared over the long grass, the rest of its toy-like frame lost in the dense fronds.

'Do we get in it or stand in the field and fly it by remote?' I demanded. Chris grinned back, understanding straightaway that this was going to be a lengthy barrage and it might be a while before we got bored.

'Bloody hell, Chris, is there a cheaper helicopter you could hire anywhere in the world?' Jeremy joined in now, just warming up.

'Look at it. Do we have to take our shoes off? Not for the carpet but to save weight. It's pitiful. I've got bigger toys on my desk.'

Chris laughed out loud and rubbed the top of his head. Clearly, he had not anticipated his treat receiving quite such a reception. But then he had probably not anticipated, when he hired it, just how small a Robinson R44 helicopter actually is when you come face to face with it.

'You've hired us a kitchen implement to go flying in, Chris. It's a Moulinex bloody helicopter. Look at it. I doubt it could whip cream.' I was getting into the swing of it now. This was going to be fun. For us.

A large man with a beard and wearing epaulettes was walking towards us now, taking awkward steps through the long grass. He was the pilot, evidently; something about his manner and his slightly defensive stance as we neared the tiny helicopter told us.

'Do we get in, mate, or shall we give you a push?'

'Where do I slot the coin to make it work?'

'How long is the flex? Don't want to get it snagged on the toaster when you take off.'

This short trip was going to seem like a very long one to Chris.

'Holy shit, he's starting it with a key!' Once again, Jeremy's voice was being fired directly into my head, only now it was through the helicopter's headsets rather than our stage earplugs. And the pilot really was slotting a car key into the dash before running through some hasty checks and firing up what sounded like a cement mixer behind us.

'Oh, stick it on a spin cycle then. Who cares about the creases?'

We were not going to let Chris off easily, even if we risked denting the pilot's pride a bit with our non-stop stream of commentary concerning the helicopter's short-comings and Chris's meanness in not shelling out for a Twin Squirrel and a fleet of hostesses to look after us. With Chris perched in the co-pilot's seat upfront and Jeremy and me squashed into the tiny rear seats, we took off and flew for a while before the pilot announced over our headsets that we were going to land again. This was okay, though, Chris assured us, all part of the plan. We would stop for lunch and then return to the theatre for the afternoon performance of our show. All very glam-orous then, and I certainly felt a twinge of excitement at the prospect of calling Mindy later to tell her that we had nipped out between shows for a helicopter flight to a restaurant. The plan dictated, of course, that our tiny hel-icopter must first land. The pilot, looking stern and strong behind his impressive beard, showed not a trace of anx-iety as he 'put the bird down' in a field of dense, lush grass surrounded by tall trees. A car was waiting for us and we were escorted off to lunch.

Returning to the helicopter some hours later, we were pleased to find that it had not been stolen.

'I mean, it could easily have been taken by a magpie in

search of something bright and spangly with which to brighten up its nest.'

'Or a child might have mistaken it for a discarded toy.'

'It could have ended up in someone's school bag.'

We were not about to let full stomachs dampen our fire when it came to heaping abuse on Chris's head today. In fact, the machine sat in the field like a stranded insect. The pilot with the manly facial hair emerged from the trees and walked towards us as we approached his craft. We clambered in. Still not saying a word, our pilot flicked a few switches, turned the key – we sniggered at this humdrum moment in the process of starting a machine still supposedly associated with glamour and excess – and began the business of taking off. I say 'began the business' because it was, as became quickly evident, a pretty involved process. It was by no means concluded thirty or forty seconds later, at which point we were still, clearly, not flying. What we were doing in fact was something more accurately described as bobbing about. We lifted into the air, hovered to about ten or twenty feet and then sank back down to the field. We lifted again, bobbed about some more, hovered to fifteen feet and sank once more to the lush grass below. And all the time the pilot shifted in his seat to look across the field, eyeing the instruments in front of him and looking up and out to the trees surrounding our field.

'Erm, is there a problem?' I asked. It was quite clear that there was indeed a problem, unless, of course, Chris had, in chartering the helicopter, also requested that we spend the afternoon hopping about an anonymous field like a

Labrador puppy trying to see over a hedge.

The pilot still didn't speak, but he lifted the machine one last time, looked out at the trees surrounding the field, glanced down at the instruments and landed again, this time with an air of finality.

'Too heavy. And too hot. It won't lift.' He looked around, pointing his manly beard at us as he spoke from behind his Aviator sunglasses in an accent as dense and thick as the beard jutting out from a chin you couldn't hurt with a baseball bat.

'What, it's broken?' Chris, by contrast with the pilot's strong tones, sounded edgy and thin.

'No, it won't lift sometimes, the air gets hot. The helicopter has been here for some hours, we are actually very high here, and we can't lift. We shall have to lose some weight.' There was not a sign of nervousness in the man or any suggestion that he found it remotely difficult to break the news to his passengers that his helicopter appeared, quite suddenly, to have turned into a garden shed. But I thought I saw his shoulders sag just a fraction under his epaulettes as he broke the news that we would have to lose weight. In actual fact, the R44 is a piston-engined helicopter and the power available from its nine-litre engine is proportionately diminished with altitude. The field in which we had parked was on high ground so we were, even when landed, at several thousand feet above sea level. The other factor affecting the power that the little helicopter was able to generate was the density of the air in which it was being asked to fly. And the density of air changed dramatically with temperature – it got less dense as it grew warmer. And it was a very, very warm day. I'm sorry if this is starting to sound like a physics lesson, but it is quite important to understand the facts that had led to Jeremy, Chris and me being forced to abandon our helicopter at this point. The field in which the pilot had landed was, as I have said, surrounded by tall trees on all sides. There were four of us on board, which is quite a weight for such a small aircraft to lift. The combination of altitude and heat robbed the helicopter of the strength to lift up vertically and climb over the trees before ascending further into the hot, blue sky. And so a plan was formed: we three would leave the helicopter and walk out of the field. The helicopter, with just the pilot on board and so relieved of most of the weight, could then take off easily, hop over the trees and land on a neighbouring stretch of ground that we could see was less compromised by foliage. We would rejoin it and then the pilot, in the new, tree-less field, could execute a running take off and all would be well. Probably.

The walk to the next field was an odd one, of course. We had been forced to abandon our helicopter and now must hope that it had the power to lift the South African pilot and his beard over the trees and land back in the long, narrow field we had selected and which, drawing upon all of our combined helicopter expertise, we declared to be an absolute cinch for take-off purposes. We heard the now familiar thunk and whirr of the tiny helicopter firing up and then, after a minute or two, a more determined thrashing sound from the blades as

Top Gear Live – people come here to watch good stuff too . . .

Well it's a living . . . I could have been an accountant.

The infamous 'tablecloth shot'. Notice the pattern of the shirt, which looks odd without ketchup stains and a salt cellar on it. Notice also the chubby-cheeked, goofy expression. I fought long and hard to eradicate this shot from the BBC's archives in order to protect my mother and my fragile, bloated TV presenter's ego. And I did it. I found it and hid it to ensure that it should never again be reproduced in print. Although I have now, of course, just reprinted it again. Bugger.

HMS *Illustrious*. Jimmy Saville never fixed this one. ➤

Illustrious gets her teeth back.

Technical, dynamic and deadly. Shortly
afterwards I got drunk, picked a fight
with a marine and tried to get into bed
with the captain.

A remarkable band of professionals in a remarkable environment.
The officers of HMS *Illustrious* – and me, spot the Wally.

it lifted and flew out of the field.

'Well there you go, it worked.'

'Yes,' said Chris, 'But technically, if we were in a heli-copter that landed and then couldn't take off again, doesn't that mean we were in a crash?'

We argued the point as we waited to be picked up and then argued it some more as we flew back to the stadium. We argued about it over a beer that evening and we were arguing about it again now, as we stood around on a helipad in Auckland and inspected the tips of the rotor blades of another, far more substantial helicopter, for bits of seagull. It made the papers, our helicopter crash. It was widely reported across the UK and beyond that we had been in involved in a crash and made a forced landing. Some went so far as to suggest that we were lucky to avoid having to ditch in the sea. One reporter turned up at my home in Herefordshire and knocked on the door in the small hours, asking a bleary-eyed Mindy how she felt about her husband, survivor of that jet car crash, now being in a helicopter crash in New Zealand last night. Mindy, needless to say, did not take this news exception-ally well and pointed out that as she had spoken to me the previous night and, indeed, that morning and I had mentioned nothing about it, then it really cannot have been much of a crash. One tends to remember such things.

Back on the helipad in Auckland, we had not been aware, as we poked and prodded at the strips of seagull flesh hanging off the rotor tips that we were, even at that moment, being photographed by the long lenses of the media and that the resulting images would be flashing back to the UK later that evening.

'I'm not sure we should stick with the helicopter thing on these tours,' said Chris, and maybe he was right; our record was not looking good. But we did stick with it and we finished our sightseeing flight that afternoon, having a lot of fun at the expense of this particular pilot, given his proven success as a butcher. He made the mistake, as we lifted out of Auckland for the second time, of confessing that this wasn't his first kill.

'Hit a sheep once, on a rough airfield.' He probably shouldn't have shared this with us, because we filled the next two hours or so with heartfelt pleas that he should be most careful to avoid crashing into that cow, or this dog or those dolphins over there. Or a whale, because they're massive and could really hurt. He doubtless got bored after a while, but had the good grace to soak it up as long as we poured it out.

We returned from our sightseeing tour without incident though and no further examples of New Zealand wildlife were cut down in the their prime by our flying machine. Strangely, despite a shaky history with the machines to date, when we returned home I took up flying helicopters myself. I fly an R44 now and, whilst I am in love with the business of operating this fiendishly complex and frighteningly clever machine, I am always conscious that the R44 I use every week, my absolute favourite machine in the entire world whose subtle curves and delicate controls I adore and revere, is exactly the same as the spindly little piece of kitchen equipment upon which we poured such scorn in South Africa. I don't mind though, it kind of helps to keep a chap's feet, sometimes literally, on the ground. And anyway, as the wounds of a few weeks earlier healed, I could reflect that helicopters would appear to be a lot safer than horses.

Chapter Ten

The Primal Scream

We don't become vain as we approach forty; it's just that there's suddenly more to worry about on the subject of how we look. A hangover no longer makes us look rugged; rather, we resemble a tramp. And each passing year advances the damage at a rate far outstripping the passage of time indicated by the calendar. In short, I'm falling apart and it's quite upsetting.

I am, it has been observed by even the less keen-eyed commentator, growing my hair long. Naturally, this extra-follicular activity has been attributed to my age and is, as I near the end of my 'approach' to forty, being seen as simply more evidence confirming that I am in the vice-like grip of a mid-life crisis. I am not. Well, yes, I am actually, massively so, but my hair isn't part of it.

This growing of the hair is simply a return to form for me; I wore my hair long for many, many years, only caving in to peer pressure and having it cut short in my early thirties in an attempt to make myself more employable. It worked; I found employment. I still have that employment, so the hair is coming back. The fact that I also wore it long in my youth and am, as I teeter on the verge of a milestone age beyond which I shall be plunged for ever into the greying ranks of the middle-aged masses, experiencing an urge to re-establish a link with those years that is stronger than the urge to eat, is of course, of some relevance. But it's not vanity, this sudden interest in my appearance, oh no. Indeed, it's driven by something else entirely, a sort of anti-vanity.

Obviously, as a television presenter I can't say that I don't care about my appearance at all. To carry on with such an attitude to my appearance would be irresponsible. I mean, there are times of the year when it's pretty difficult to turn a telly on without me lumbering out of it into your living room to waffle on about cars, people falling off obstacle courses, science or some such stuff. And if I were to neglect my appearance to such an extent that I left parts of it uncovered that are best tucked away, or allowed moss to grow across my head, then I would risk causing people genuine offence and deserve to be prosecuted or persecuted for so doing.

Even so, please take a moment to consider how awful it would be on pretty much a daily basis if I were to be uncomfortable with seeing myself. Well, clearly not as bad as it is for the legions of people who switch on their telly hoping for something illuminating, exciting or funny and are presented yet again with the spectacle of that short bloke off *Top Gear* goofing about. But, nevertheless, I ask you to consider how tricky it would be for me if the sight of myself were to provoke a response along the lines of that exhibited by lots of people upon seeing themselves appear in, say, a holiday video. If every time anyone turned on the telly I were to shriek and howl and remark how fat I looked or that I never realised my ears were that big, life would quickly prove unbearable.

And so, yes, I have been obliged by circumstance to nurture a kind of immunity to the sight of myself; it doesn't cause me undue distress to see from the TV screen that I am, in fact, quite short, that from some angles my gut sticks out beyond my pigeon chest and that I really must remember not to slouch. It is, though, a sizeable leap from learning not to scream, hoot and panic at the sight of oneself to taking a genuine interest in the business of how we look. I did once and, if I'm honest, it caused me more trouble than it was worth.

✳

It wasn't that I wished the woman ill, as she cowered behind a large metal filing cabinet; it was just that I was frustrated. My visit to the picture library somewhere deep inside the BBC had been motivated by months of growing anger, frustration and embarrassment following the regular appearance in newspapers and magazines of a particular photograph of me. While not a compromising photograph in the vein of those involving politicians, special rubber underclothes and fruit bowls, this partic-ular shot had, nevertheless, been causing considerable consternation in the Hammond household. It is a fairly standard head and shoulders shot taken, in fact, on our first ever day at the brand new Top Gear studio back in

2002. But in it I appear to have the chubby, red-cheeked, button-nosed face of a character out of *Alice in Wonderland* and am wearing a 1950s tablecloth as a shirt and a grin so smug you could spread it on toast. It was, upon the announcement of my joining the team for the relaunched *Top Gear* programme, widely distributed by the BBC as my official photograph and had been lodged in their files to be issued upon request for an image of me by the publishing world.

The photograph had shown its ugly face – well, my ugly face – in newspapers, magazines and TV listings on a number of occasions and on each one I had opened whatever rag it was printed in to be confronted with this same disappointing image and then braced myself for a barrage of calls from friends, relatives, colleagues and business associates pointing out that I appeared to be putting on a bit of weight in the chins department and asking why I had confused my shirt with my table linen. When I say 'barrage' it is not understating the matter; the phone would ring continuously from the moment of the picture's first appearance to the moment of its first being used to wrap chips or line a budgie's cage. When I say that the callers were 'friends, relatives, colleagues and business associates,' however, I am being not entirely candid. They were limited, in fact, to relatives. Well, specifically, they were limited to one relative; the callers were all my mother.

This photograph would cause such a seismic tremor on the otherwise smooth countenance of my mother that I could, wherever I was in the world, sense the very second that her eyes fell upon it and then anticipate the subsequent wave of white-hot anger radiating from her like an electro-magnetic pulse and be ready to pick up the phone and do the filial pouring oil on troubled waters bit. I had always been rather charmed by this sensitivity on the part of my mother towards this particular image of her son. It made me feel cared about and nurtured; it made me feel, in fact, like a son. And that's a great thing.

My mother has plenty of things to be doing in the course of running her own business and dealing with her ever-growing fleet of eight grandchildren, but, nevertheless, if during her brief coffee break or on a train journey into London she opened a newspaper or a magazine to see this particular photograph of her eldest son looking like a nursery rhyme character poking his fat head through a tablecloth, she would never hesitate to find the time in her busy schedule to fly off the handle and demonstrate a little of the kind of old-school indignant mother's anger that made this country great. This pudgy little lump of modelling clay wrapped in table linen was certainly not her eldest son and I rather formed the impression that she wasn't entirely comfortable with the idea of the world thinking it was.

Having poured oil on the troubled, I would generally ring the BBC press office responsible for issuing the photograph to the media and bleat at them down the phone to the effect that there must, surely, be a slightly less damning photograph of me that they might issue instead. Now, this whole problem was, inevitably, exacerbated by my being under the universal male illusion that I bear a striking resemblance to Johnny Depp, Clint Eastwood and Brad Pitt, all at the same time. No male wants to be in possession of a pair of velvety, chubby cheeks, a softly defined, downy chin and a jaw that serves really only to connect those same cheeks with the thin neck below rather than make an angular statement of virility, potency and jutting manliness. And so those of us whose face rather conforms to the whole velvety-soft, slightly chubby aesthetic – that is to say, nearly all of us – simply choose not to believe the evidence of our own eyes.

This is easy when looking in, say, a shaving mirror. For one thing, it's usually pretty early in the morning when we set about scraping the chin and so any tendency of the cheek towards chubbiness or of the jaw towards softness can be blamed on early morning bleariness in the eyes department. Spend a couple of decades or so staring blearily into the mirror of a morning to scrape the nocturnal fuzz off your chin while persuading yourself that what you see right now is not necessarily what the rest of the world will see when you descend the stairs and face them later, and pretty soon the illusion is complete. When confronted, therefore, with a photograph of ourselves that fails to correspond with the image lodged in our heads, we simply question the accuracy of the photograph. And on this occasion, it would seem that I had a point. My mother agreed with my condemnation of the photograph as being nothing like me – albeit from a slightly biased standpoint in her case, as my mother – and this was enough to motivate me to action.

On my next visit to London, buoyed up by a sense of righteous indignation in defence of my mother's wounded sensitivity, I popped into the BBC's publicity department with the intention of expunging the offending photograph from their library and seeing that it was replaced with one more accurately reflecting the finely chiselled features that I knew, in reality, I presented to the world. I stormed into what I had learned from the receptionist was the correct office and stood among the usual bland furniture and potted plants and complained loudly and stridently. While the librarian hid behind a filing cabinet, I delivered my pre-rehearsed lines about how 'you wouldn't bloody well like it if there was a picture of you looking like that out there and people kept printing it in the world's media, would you?' The librarian blinked, her eyes huge behind thick glasses and her long fingers sticking to the sides of the cabinet behind which she hid as though she might just flee up it like a gecko. I coaxed her out into the open.

'Absolutely. Don't know how it got there. I'll take it out and replace it.' She spoke earnestly, with a surprisingly low voice. I hadn't prepared myself to be faced with this immediate and friendly capitulation and it rather took the furious wind out of my sail.

I followed her across the room towards another bank of filing cabinets. She slid open a drawer and pulled from it slowly, as though withdrawing a medical vial containing some dreadful virus, a clear plastic sheet with many pouches, each holding a 35mm transparency. We moved back across the room, slowly and with precision, to a table on which sat a white, rectangular box about the height of a shoe box and the width of a kitchen sink. She extended a long finger and slowly stabbed a switch at the base of the box, the surface of which flickered with light. It was a light box, by means of which the librarian could examine the transparencies she had pulled from the filing cabinet. Now she held the plastic sheet over the light and ran a finger slowly across it before selecting a particular transparency and sliding the small, white square from its pocket. She smiled slowly and almost fondly, lowering the transparency on to the light box. In the tiny rectangle of coloured light, I saw the familiar chubby cheeks, the vacuous smile and the red-checked shirt and shuddered, reaching instinctively for my phone ready for my mother's call. But, of course, she couldn't see it today and, as this was the master, neither would she see it again. I thanked the picture librarian and bowed out of the office.

It was at least a week before the picture appeared again. Some newspaper or other had written a piece about a film I had made about the Gunpowder Plot and there, among the words, was the familiar, gurning, fat-faced picture of me looking strangely smug and pleased with myself for wearing a shirt that had clearly, until only moments before, served as a barrier between ketchup bottle and table. I explained to my mother that I had actually visited the picture library to see it removed and really didn't understand how it could still be putting in an appearance over her morning slice of toast to spoil her day.

But, of course, the newspapers themselves keep their own libraries of photographs ready for action in the TV listings pages or to accompany stories about how so and so has fallen out of a nightclub drunk and been sick on a minor royal. The Chubby Checker shot – for so the image had been called on account of its fat-faced rendition of me in a pink and white checked shirt – was still out there, lodged in the filing cabinet of a hundred newspapers and magazines; a ticking bomb ready to explode and ruin my breakfast at any moment. And there was nothing more I could do, short of donning a superhero costume and targeting newspaper offices by night to break in, rifle through their picture library and take away their copy. It would keep me on my toes at least.

The 'Chubby Checker' did put in a few more surprise appearances over the ensuing year or two. And my mother's response to the sight of it remained predictably explosive and to me, at least, strangely comforting. But we reached a point where I might open a magazine or a newspaper, turn a page or two, only to be confronted by it yet again, perhaps next to an advertisement for a programme I had made or a feature about my love of bicycles or celery, and when I reached for my phone ready to receive my mother's furious call it never came. And, strangely, I found my own reaction to it mellowing. It really wasn't so bad, in fact. From some angles, the thing looked jaunty, quite friendly and tinged by a sort of open cheeriness. There were far worse photographs of me lurking about the place.

Indeed, I had noticed a phenomenon recently whereby

I would, at the request of some publication or other, visit a photographer's studio to stand there in the time-honoured fashion and gurn at the flashlight, only to have the photographer's sincere and heartfelt assurances that all was going really well and that the photograph would be an absolute cracker prove as hollow as an empty biscuit tin when the resulting image finally appeared in whatever magazine had commissioned it.

Time after time this happened. Despite the photographer issuing compliments and reassurances at a rate that would leave a Monte Carlo watch salesman looking rude and churlish, the photograph that appeared in the press would show someone clearly other than me. I raved and shouted about it, asking the heavens above why it was that these blokes couldn't just wheel me in to their stupid studio and stop messing about with choosing which 'inspirational' music track to play or what species of olive to order for lunch and just concentrate on taking a snap that showed me as I really am rather than the tired, hollow-eyed little man whose picture they sent in to the editor. I grew tired of making phone calls to the picture desks – just as I rather fear they may have grown tired of receiving them – to point out that the photograph they had taken had come out all wrong for some reason and that I wasn't very pleased at all.

The realisation did not come at any specific moment, or at least not one that I can recall. Though I may have erased the horror of that moment from my memory banks and proceeded under the illusion that it happened gradually when really it landed like a hammer blow that propelled me to my knees soundlessly before I tilted my head back to issue forth a primal scream so ripe with horror that it sent birds thundering from the trees hundreds of miles away and stopped traffic in cities across the world. Either way, the fact is that it finally occurred to me that some of the mistakes on these shots – the eye bags, the wrinkles, the creased brow, spare chin, scraggy neck and curling eyebrows – were in fact faithful reproductions of what actually sat in front of the lens. That is to say, the realisation that dawned on me – slowly or otherwise – was that it wasn't the photographs at fault; it was the image in my head. A significant moment, I'm sure you will agree.

It took some sinking in. But once sunk, it has made some things an awful lot easier to understand. It had always struck me as rather odd that, as little Richard Hammond from Shirley, I should find myself responsible for two daughters, married to a grown woman, paying a mortgage and driving about the place, quite legally, in a car. Now, though, with the help of this new understanding, I have got it: I'm a grown-up. And when a chap finally says that, finally accepts his adulthood as a reality and not still a distant possibility beckoning to him through the testosterone-soaked drapes of his teenage years, it really means something. And among the many things it means to me is that if I want my hair long, I shall bloody well wear it long. It's not vanity, far from it, in fact: it's the dawn of realisation that I really don't have to worry about how I look because I am a grown-up. Some of life's battles are etched across my face, many of life's larger dinners are indicated around my midriff and if I want to wear my hair long, who's going to tell me to have it cut? It is anti-vanity and I am very, very comfortable with it.

Chapter Eleven

A Childhood Dream

Looking out of the rain-streaked window of the massive Sikorsky helicopter, I watched the grey rectangle of the ship's deck, like a roof slate, a few hundred feet below us, toiling through the North Sea. The ship was HMS *Illustrious*, an aircraft carrier, and when I set foot on deck – in about ten minutes' time – it would be the realisation of a long-held ambition. This was something I had always wanted to do. I may, in fact, have written to Jimmy Savile on the subject many years before, although this does not necessarily mark it out as an entirely unique ambition to lodge itself in my head as a child, because I also wrote to Sir Jimmy asking if he might possibly arrange for me to drive a long-wheel-base Land Rover. He never did – which always struck me as rather mean, given that he facilitated the realisation of dreams and wishes of a far more ambitious nature for fleets of young people on a weekly basis.

I have gone on about this before, I know, but, deep in the Hammond breast, it still rankles. Every weekend I would watch as some dough-faced young ballet dancer pranced out on to the stage with the Royal Ballet, or some jug-eared young hooligan landed a fighter jet and wrestled with the actual Batman. All Sir Jimmy had to do to bring about the realisation of the dream that tugged at the imagination of this young boy was call up the factory in Lode Lane, ask to borrow a demonstrator and slot the young stripling into it for five minutes to tootle about on some deserted airfield with no innocent bystanders or items of street furniture put at risk and only the tiniest of dents inflicted upon the purse so generously donated to the BBC by the licence fee paying public. He could have set that one up in his tea break. But, no: he chose to let me down and I had to watch as my dreams were dashed against the treacherous rocks of the TV ratings war. And, sadly, Sir Jimmy never fixed it for me to walk on the deck of an aircraft carrier either, but no matter, because, thirty years later, as I stepped out of the helicopter and lowered a shoe, my dream came true anyway and I took my first steps on to the vast and slowly rolling deck.

The weather was behaving in a manner entirely appropriate for a chap's first visit to one of Her Majesty's warships and I grinned as the wind whipped needles of rain across my face and tugged at my waxed jacket. I was aware that a Barbour shooting jacket is not standard issue in Royal Navy circles, but I was not in possession of a set of oilskins and the only alternative I could find while packing my stuff at home the previous night had been a rather lurid green skiing jacket that turned up in a box of stuff in the garage having come into my possession from

God knows where but that was of a colour ordinarily indicative of a gastric emergency and not, I felt, appropriate for the trip. I tugged at the thin, greasy collar and tried my best to huddle down into my Barbour as, around me, the assembled members of Her Majesty's Royal Navy greeted the TV crew and director.

I sucked in a lungful or two of the cold, salty air and felt pretty jolly all round. This opportunity to fulfil a childhood dream had come about, once again, in the course of my work. We were there to spend four days on board, filming an episode of *Engineering Connections* featuring the ship itself. On the brief flight over from Newcastle, I had pondered how it might feel to walk across the deck of such a vast creature, to feel it rolling beneath my feet. And as the heavy blades of the Sikorsky thrashed above us and chewed up the winter sky, I had fallen into one of those slightly soulful and hugely self-indulgent states of mind where one rather tends to mess about with things best left under their respective mental stones, undisturbed. This trip was, I decided, very important to me. It managed, in fact, to bracket two distinct and significant parts of my life. Well, I did warn you that I had rather dropped through a hole in the smooth surface of my consciousness and ended up rummaging about in some of the more hopeless and embarrassingly soulful regions beneath ...

The point was, I had concluded after ten minutes or so of resting chin in hand and staring gloopily out of the window like a homesick Labrador, that, while it was as a ten-year-old boy that I was first caught up wildly by the idea of these huge and exciting floating cities, I was finally afforded the opportunity to realise my dream of visiting one just as I left behind not only my childhood, but also my young adulthood and graduated into the realms of what must be regarded – and I sighed like a lovesick teenager as I confessed this to myself – as middle age. I resolved to comfort myself with the dignity and statesman-like behaviour expected of someone approaching his fortieth birthday. I would, I decided, apply the lessons I had learned over the past year – many of which have already been discussed in these pages. This, then, was my chance to put it all together. And so, in a poetic and really quite beautiful piece of circularity, I would, in the course of achieving a childhood dream, finally enter adulthood. And then I snapped myself out of this cringeworthy bout of soppy self-indulgence to engage in some manly banter with the bloke operating the winch about whether it would ever be sturdy enough to lower the director down to the deck on account of him being such a fat bastard.

And, shortly afterwards, we landed. Those two words do encompass rather a lot of business, in fact, because the task of landing a helicopter on the deck of a moving ship is an involved and fiddly one. I fly a helicopter myself and have found that, even when landing on a rock-steady field on a dead calm day, there is more than enough to occupy the two hands and two feet with which our maker chose to equip us – failing to foresee, perhaps, the necessity of being in possession of at least six of each when controlling a helicopter. As the TV crew busied themselves hooking things up, inserting tapes, checking clipboards and swapping impenetrable jargon, I watched in awe as the grizzled chap up front slewed the huge machine around in a giant, clattering arc and held us in a steady hover over a deck that appeared to me to be moving far, far more than the deck of what is essentially a floating town ever should move. Eventually he lowered us down until the wheels kissed the deck to execute a softer, more graceful landing than I have ever achieved on the entirely predictable and reliable surface of Gloucester Airport.

As we gathered around the broad door in the side of the Sikorsky and readied ourselves to exit, I became suddenly conscious that the TV crew bore with them their cameras, lens boxes, tripods, filter cases, sound mixers, boom poles, lights, tapes, spare tapes, extra tapes, spare batteries and power cables. Traditionally, television presenters have only two items of kit with which to concern themselves. These are a script, so that they know what to say, and a mobile telephone with which to telephone their agent when they can't remember how much they are being paid. On this occasion, though, as I prepared myself to take these significant first steps into a dream and, effectively, into adulthood, I thought it a good idea to demonstrate a greater degree of sincerity and depth of character than might traditionally be associated with the presenter on such an occasion and grabbed a blue holdall I found lying with a mass of silver flight cases.

There was a stifled yelp amid the racket from the helicopter.

'That's my bag, sir.' It was the winch man who raised his voice in a manly bellow over the noise from the engines, as the blades still whipped about overhead, to address me from the other side of the machine. 'Only got my smalls in, I'm afraid. Unless you need it?' He grinned and held out a hand to retrieve his kitbag from me.

'Ah, yes. Heavy, isn't it,' I shouted back and passed it over. He hefted it into a corner of the helicopter as easily as he might throw a screwed-up paper bag into a bin.

'I'm away for a while, sir. Need a fair bit of kit.'

'I see. Yes.'

Anxious still to demonstrate to the world that I am a man happy to muck in with the crew and get the job done, I reached for a second, smaller bag from the dwindling pile by the door, having first checked with an inquisitive look and a raised eyebrow aimed at the cameraman to confirm that this was part of our filming equipment and not a sack of emergency flares or the pilot's lunch. He returned the look with an affirmative nod and I picked up the bag. It was heavier than the sun.

'Bloody hell. We started carrying a spare collapsed star around with us then? Just in case?' I yelled out to the cameraman who grinned back as I staggered under the weight of it as the bag's thin blue nylon handles threatened to slice straight through my knuckles and leave my severed fingers flapping on the floor of the helicopter. The cameraman yelled something back, but it was lost to the noise as the sound from the engines built to a sudden crescendo and then settled into a piercing drone as the pilot lowered the revs to let it cool before shutting down.

And now I stood on the deck, my childhood dream fulfilled, wearing an inappropriate but rather stylish waxed jacket and wondering if I should bluster up to the chap who appeared to be in charge or wait until I was ushered into his presence to introduce myself. They were likely to be a bit keen on tradition and formality around these parts, from what I knew of naval types, and I didn't want to begin my time on board by dropping some almighty social clanger. This, remember, was my chance to really pull together the lessons I had learned in my approach to forty and I was keen to behave accordingly. I chose to wait for the introductions and looked about me instead. The deck stretched away in all directions, massive, dull, grey and oddly menacing. The white markings to guide aircraft and other vehicles created the illusion that this was a road. In fact, it was like standing on a major road junction in the middle of the sea. Naturally, it came to an abrupt end around the edges and, beyond it, I watched the North Sea heave itself about.

This was not, we had been told by the helicopter crew, a big sea, not by any stretch of the imagination, and I was amazed to see how much the deck still rolled and pitched. This, then, was the real deal, a warship built for battle and heroic adventures on the high seas. I kept a keen eye out for bicycles, having learned as a child that sailors on board these vast, seagoing airports would use them as transport about the huge, windswept decks. I didn't see any bicycles, but further along the deck a man wearing a set of dark blue overalls and what, from the bulk and serious look of it, could only be an official Royal Navy-issue waterproof coat, was manoeuvring a small, squat vehicle with what sounded like a diesel engine chuntering away inside it. I guessed that it was some sort of tug for the purposes of moving aircraft about the place and I wondered how easy such a task might be when the weather really put its back into it and sent the big ship bouncing around on the waves like a cork in the bath.

Snapping, once again, out of a reverie, I rejoined the main group by the helicopter and introduced myself to what appeared to be the senior chap among them. Handshakes and convivial greetings were exchanged and, despite the weather, a warm and friendly atmosphere suffused the place. As we chatted and moved through the first exchanges that follow such an introduction, a crew member hove-to at my elbow – probably best to avoid using nautical phraseology, I figured, but I could at least run it in my head for personal enjoyment – and introduced himself. We enjoyed some banter about the ship and the weather and he said something else that I missed. I asked him to repeat it, blaming the gusts of wind. I caught the windblown words the fourth time.

'You've got something on your shoe.'

'Sorry?'

'Stuck to your shoe. Some tape or something.'

I looked down and could see nothing. The man smiled kindly and pointed to my right leg – keen, it would appear, to warn me of some wardrobe malfunction that might cause me embarrassment or even danger on the treacherous decks of a working warship.

'Thanks.' I bent my leg at the knee and lifted the shoe away from the deck and backwards so that I might turn my head and look down on the sole. And with one voice, the ten or eleven members of the ship's crew standing around me shouted, 'Hello, sailor!'

Lesson one about life aboard an aircraft carrier as a civilian, then; they quite like a laugh when the opportunity presents itself.

It was, with hindsight, perhaps obvious that a visit to the Senior Rates Mess might contain within it the opportunity for more laughs to be had at the expense of the visiting TV presenter. I didn't have the benefit of hindsight, though, and blundered into the experience expecting to pass a pleasant evening in the company of the men and women serving aboard just the kind of mighty vessel that had cruised through my childhood dreams. They were certainly a most friendly and accommodating bunch. As I wandered the decks on my first day, a constant stream of warm and friendly 'hellos' and 'good mornings' had greeted me. At first I thought this might be a natural reaction to seeing a new face on board, particularly when that face is one off the telly. And then I had stopped on a corner and heard the same greetings and enquiries after health and wellbeing being exchanged at every meeting. On narrow stairways, in cramped corners and on exposed gantries, every encounter between two or more people was peppered with friendly chat. And I realised that this was part of a culture that had evolved very much out of necessity. People serving aboard a warship will spend huge amounts of time together and therefore getting along is essential if life is to remain bearable. But this is about more than the occasional game of drafts and remembering someone's birthday. As the crew of a warship, they may have to go to war together and will rely on one another in the most life and death situations imaginable. And so, not surprisingly, there exists a bond between crew members unlike any other and the constant stream of happy banter and greetings seems just a way of keeping that bond functioning and ready for the times when it is needed in very different circumstances. I had pointed out to the captain, in fact, when invited to join him for breakfast on the bridge on the first morning I spent on board, that the ship was indeed the most friendly and polite place I think I had ever been. It was, I declared, like spending a few days in the Cotswolds. And then I looked past him across the wind-lashed decks at the grey, hunched shape of a military helicopter and the stark, functional edges of the flight deck. Well, maybe not exactly like the Cotswolds then.

And on this particular evening I had been invited to the Senior Rates Mess. Peering into a narrow mirror in my small, slowly rolling cabin, I adjusted my borrowed tie and not for the first time experienced a twinge of awkwardness and a pang of regret over my decision to bring only jeans for this trip. Jeans, it seemed, were frowned upon in the Officers' Mess and I had experienced a slightly tricky moment when I first launched myself through the door, wobbly legs shrouded in the familiar blue denim. Those officers present had raised eyebrows at the appearance of someone not observing the dress code but refrained from commenting, out of politeness no doubt. When I did eventually ask if it was acceptable to wear jeans in what was, clearly, a smart, formal area, I uncorked the hole in the dam and the hitherto restrained lake of objections flooded over me; no, it was not acceptable; yes, I had broken the rules; no, they wouldn't expect better from a civilian really, especially one working in telly; and, yes, I should be keel-hauled. Anyway, did I want a drink? In actual fact, the inappropriate leg wear turned out to be an excellent icebreaker.

Tonight, though, I was slated for a drink with the Senior Rates and their mess would welcome me in my jeans, apparently. And at least I had shirt and tie for the top half, so a compromise had been reached. A junior officer specially selected for the duty guided me through the decks to the mess. A guide is, it turned out, pretty essential in such circumstances, an aircraft carrier being a tricky thing to navigate for, I should imagine, the first ten years or so until one has grown accustomed to it. As we descended yet another steep set of what looked at first glance to be stairs but proved, on closer inspection, to be ladders, I determined to have a word with the captain, should I be invited to breakfast again. I would point out that these warships were all well and good and that I was sure lots of chaps with slide rules in their nautical pockets and pencils behind their ears were involved in designing one, but that anything could be improved and I had a few suggestions for this particular ship.

As we threaded our way along a narrow corridor and began our descent of a third and final ladder, I considered how much better the place could be if they had only made the ship some ten or twenty metres longer and given all the stairs a gentler gradient. Also, I would tell the captain over a bowl of cornflakes and a mug of the best, a lot fewer sharp edges would help make life more comfortable. Having banged elbows and knees several times against corners that were, in my opinion, unnecessarily sharp and hard, I could see how many of them could be rounded off with a gentle radius and even padded with some soft material of a neutral hue.

We reached the required deck, walked another few metres of corridor, and I was shown into the Senior Rates Mess. It was a room of no particular style, just plain walls, tables, soft chairs and a television screen. While well-equipped and, no doubt, functional to the umpteenth degree, I would say with confidence that no one with fancy glasses and a retail outlet in London's King's Road had been involved in styling the place. And I liked it immediately. I was greeted warmly, of course, and settled into a large group around a table. Drinks were called for, and, after a couple of beers and much amiable chatter about life in the navy and life in television, it was suggested that I try a tot of Pusser's Rum. The suggestion was met with much warmth by the assembled group and I conceded happily that, yes, I'd give it a go.

Pusser's Rum, I would discover later, after the worst of the pain had gone and I could see again, acquired its name from Purser's Rum. Every rating in the Royal Navy was issued with a daily serving of rum, a 'tot', and the particular spirit used was a blend of different rums from all over the world. It has many fine qualities; the taste is considered velvety and complex, and you can almost catch the Jamaican breezes as it flows through you. But uppermost among these fine qualities is its strength – almost 55 per cent alcohol by volume.

I knew none of these facts as the glass was placed before me, but became aware of a sense of expectation building around the room as the rum was poured. Another thing of which I was blissfully unaware at this stage was the official size of the original naval tot of rum. It was, in fact, an eighth of a pint. However, the pourer that day must have been feeling especially generous towards his fellow man, because the measure sloshed into the thick glass in front of me amounted to something nearer a third of a pint.

Now I am, as has been pointed out on more than one occasion, not the largest of chaps. There is, all told, probably no more than 70kgs of me, standing barely 5 foot 7 inches off the ground on a good day. And so the natural assumption would be, no doubt, that I am possessed of the drinking prowess of a mother superior. However, the Hammond constitution is made of much, much sterner stuff and I am, for whatever reason, blessed with an ability to soak up the electric water at a rate prodigious and committed enough to fell many a man three times my size. What helps here, no doubt, was a two-year spell during which, having finally grown tired of working at a selection of radio stations for pay cheques that could afford me no better lifestyle than living in a single-room bedsit and limiting myself to the bicycle for transport, I put my blossoming media career on hold, pinned a 'For Sale' sign to my soul, and moved over into PR.

Working in PR, while pretty much putting the kibosh on one's chances of sailing though the Pearly Gates without creating a bit of a stir among the bouncers, does bring certain advantages compared with hosting the late-night talk show on a local radio station. For one thing, there is the money; quite a lot of it by comparison with the few coins I was accustomed to throwing into the bottomless pit of my overdraft each month. But foremost among these good things was the opportunity to develop, on company expenses, a cast-iron liver and the ability to drink even a Viking under the table.

I became a press officer. I never did quite understand the sense of rank and status brought about by the title of 'officer'; I didn't get a badge of rank or anything and no one ever called me sir. But the journalists it was my job to haul about the place were very polite to me, respectful even. This was because I had a company credit card and we were, during these bouts of polite respectfulness, generally in a bar. It was my job, as far as I could make out, to buy drinks all night and I became really rather good at it. I could buy drinks from six in the evening until six in the morning. I would stay at the bar, leaning earnestly on the counter and listening to the journalists' stories and bad jokes until the last one of them finally crawled off to bed or wilted like an autumn leaf and curled up under a table.

Of course, my job then required that I should also be first up in the morning to greet the entirely different species of journalist who would, upon arrival the previous evening at whatever hotel was hosting this particular beano, have hurled themselves into the swimming pool to knock off a few hundred lengths before retiring to their room to spend the night filing words to their newspaper. By six in the morning, they would have finished whatever in-depth piece of analysis they had been penning, visited the gym for an hour or so and be ready to present themselves at breakfast where they would expect to be entertained over their bowl of muesli and soya milk by an enthusiastic company press officer of bright eye and bushy tail. I would have prepared for this ordeal by drinking steadily until five or six in the morning and so, with all the brightness of eye and bushiness of tail I could muster after a fifteen-minute sleep and a shower, I would breeze into the restaurant and regale this second batch of journalists with wit, knowledge and insightful remarks.

It came a bit hard at first and I was relieved, frankly, if I got away with the whole process each time without actually being sick on someone. Nevertheless, over time I improved until I really could stay up with the night owls and get up with the earliest of the early birds. There is no secret to this, no magic formula or hangover cure or pre-session menu. It is, like any other skill, only achievable through hard practice and dedication. After a year as a press officer, I was in peak condition and at the very top of my game. This, though, was nearly fifteen years ago and I do, on occasion, forget to take this into consideration and, as a result, run the risk of over-reaching myself.

✳

I eyed the glass of rum. Around me, the Rates were cheering and laughing, confident, I was sure, that this tot would be beyond this short, skinny TV bloke. I picked it up; the glass itself was heavy, weighed down further by what I now reckoned to be nearer to half a pint of super-strength rum. No problem; I could deal with this and it would be a chance to demonstrate that not everyone in telly was a soft lightweight surrounded by yes-men and stylists. I rolled my head on my neck, a few of the Rates sensed that I was going for it and quietened down. While I would not go so far as to say that an actual hush descended on the room, there was, nevertheless, an air of expectation among my companions. I smiled confidently and downed the contents, placing the glass firmly back down on the table with smart 'click' and commenting that the rum was good. And it was good, too, strong but rich in flavour. I'm not a connoisseur of rum, but this tasted like decent stuff. Within seconds, my glass had been refilled and placed in front of me.

'Now steady, lads, I know it would be funny to get the bloke off the telly drunk, but I've got to work tomorrow and, y'know, I'm only here for a few days. Can't overdo it.' I lifted the glass anyway, confident that I had every-thing under control, and necked it. My confidence after that point, by all subsequent accounts, grew considerably. It grew to the extent that I identified and attempted to start a fight with the largest marine on the ship. A big bloke, he was content to restrain me gently and point out, according to those of my own film crew who watched the spectacle, that he was really rather good at this sort of thing, fighting, and that I would be better off sitting back down and not being so silly. According, once again, to my crew, much pacified and mollified by the man's tone, I decided at this point to retire to my bed. I thanked the crowd for their hospitality and generosity, repeated my assurances that, yes, I was fine and not in the slightest bit affected by the Pusser's Rum and set off for my cabin.

An aircraft carrier is, as I have been keen to stress, a most fantastically enormous thing and the maze of corridors, passageways and decks it contains are enough to boggle the clearest of minds. Mine, unfortunately, was not the clearest of minds by this stage and, as I set off confidently up the stairs, the marine with whom I had, according to reports, been trying to start some sort of boxing match, felt it best to follow me at a discreet distance to make sure I found my way back to my temporary home.

It must be true, the marine's story, because it was told me by so many different people the following day that the amount of cross-checking and coordination required to get such a thing off the ground as a lie among the large, close-knit community of a warship would have been beyond even Her Majesty's Royal Navy. And the story ran that I reached the upper levels of the ship, took a wrong turning or two and was stopped by the marine as I extended an arm and lurched forwards through the door to the captain's cabin. Upon being so stopped, I insisted that this was, in fact, my cabin but was finally dissuaded of that view by the marine, who took the precaution of escorting me back to my own bunk and encouraging me to sleep it off, ready for a busy new day.

The naval tot was abandoned in 1970, with the tradition given a fine send-off on many ships. In an act of gritty defiance and romantic symbolism probably rather typical of the navy, some crews chose to sling their last tot over the side and others gave their ship's official rum barrel a burial at sea. Had such a burial been made available to me on this particular morning, I would have been over the side faster than a torpedo and heading for Davy Jones's locker with a sense of relief and gratitude larger than the ship I had left behind. As it was, I contented myself with leaning against anything that came within leaning range and working slowly and steadily through the morning's work, taking solace from the fact that I hadn't actually been sick on anyone and would probably survive until the evening.

My opportunity to Put It All Together and enter middle age with a mature and sensible flourish had been presented to me and I had made a mess of it. But at least, I figured, as I lowered myself into my bunk later that night, I had demonstrated consistency; there was no doubting that the bloke who, as a teenager, rode his motorcycle around Ripon and covered his leather jacket in silver studs was the same bloke who arrived on an aircraft carrier to make a TV programme, picked a fight with the biggest marine on board and tried to get into bed with the captain. I smiled as I drifted off to sleep on my narrow bunk. It hurt.

The following day brought about a transformation on board that was marked enough to have me wondering if I might accidentally have stumbled on to the wrong ship on my way back from the heads – sorry, lavatories; one can't help sometimes slipping back into the old naval lingo. It's often that way with us old salts. Anyway, as I wandered the decks and hooked up with my film crew ready for our third day of filming the links and sequences that would make up our TV show, I felt rather than saw or heard this change at first. There was a sense of tension vibrating in the air. The same polite and friendly 'hellos' and 'good mornings' were exchanged, but the people exchanging them were acting with a subtle sense of urgency and purpose that I had not picked up on before. As we moved about the ship, I saw groups of young officers mustered together at what looked like significant points, carrying equipment and clipboards.

Eventually, I asked what was going on and was told that the Harriers were coming in today. I had, of course, noticed that on this particular aircraft carrier the actual aircraft appeared to be conspicuously absent from the place. Apart from the massive helicopter that had delivered the crew and me on board, I had seen neither a wing nor a rotor since embarking. I had wondered at first if they might have some large, secret cupboard into which the fighters could all be tidied away for convenience and security. But, no, they were due to fly in and land aboard today and for the crew of HMS *Illustrious* it was a moment laden with enough significance to, well, to sink a battleship. They had been without their planes for months now as they had been deployed to war zones elsewhere. And as I wandered the decks, I heard crew members talking excitedly of how good it would be for the ship to get her 'teeth' back. After all, what is an aircraft carrier without aircraft?

Naturally, we would be filming their arrival; it promised to be a spectacle few are privileged to see at first hand and would make for valuable and exciting footage in our film. And naturally, too, I was as excited as a ten-year-old on Christmas Eve. I found myself tuning into the general air of controlled tension on board; I looked anxiously out of every opening on to the deck as we passed, half expecting to see the sky black with approaching fighter jets. It slowly became clear that there were teams of people on board whose lives revolved around the aircraft themselves and so they would suddenly have their function, their status and their pride back as they managed the landing, stowing and preparation in readiness for immediate deployment of the aircraft.

As the hour of the Harriers' arrival approached, the action grew more intense, though it still took place at the same measured, tautly controlled pace. Men and women in heavy-duty waterproofs and brightly coloured ear muffs strode about the deck, checking things. Large pieces of functional, seriously practical machinery were moved about and readied to do whatever it was that they would do. We filmed the preparations and, as we did so, found our own tension levels rising with the excitement that now fizzed through every deck and corner of the ship.

And when they did arrive, screaming in from a leaden, grey sky like demons, the aircraft brought with them a heroic sense of just what an aircraft carrier is about. Routines clicked into action as the planes landed vertically on the deck and were marshalled into place. We watched from a gantry up on the superstructure, looking down on the suddenly busy deck. The noise was beyond anything I have ever heard or, more importantly, felt. Because you *do* feel it. It resonates and vibrates through every deck of the vast ship; a physical manifestation of the tensions and excitement that had buzzed through those same decks all morning in anticipation of the return of the ships' treasured 'teeth'. And what teeth they were: the blunt, stubby Harriers, roaring down on to the deck, bellies exposed to the view of the hundreds waiting to welcome them aboard.

What looked to be almost the entire ship's company had turned out, not surprisingly, to share in this significant and important reunion of aircraft carrier and aircraft. As the first of them made the committed lunge on to the deck and bounced down on to its tiny wheels to sit, hunched like a lethal insect, I will confess to a goose bump or two. These fast, deadly things had buzzed home to roost. The comparisons with wasps' nests, beehives or eagles' nests whirled around my head in a blizzard of noise and stark imagery. The Harriers' dull, angular forms were outlined sharply against the steely sea glinting beyond the deck.

As the final planes slammed down on to the deck, I admired the commitment of the pilots as they passed the point of no return and went for it. Harrier pilots fly alone; it is their job to fly the plane and operate its weapons system. And I wondered how busy they must be at this point in any mission. They are home, in effect, but those last few feet back to the sanctuary look to be as frantic and critical as a battle manoeuvre in their own right. Once they have begun their vertical descent, they cannot change their mind and take off again. Each pilot must be guided to his allotted slot on deck and then it is down to him to choose the specific second on which to put the plane down. And, once taken, that decision cannot be changed.

The landings seemed, at first, to be worryingly heavy. This is because of this business of not being able to take off again at that point. And so, if they are to land, they must commit to it, do it and do it just once. Watching the first one perform its trademark heavy landing, I feared it might crash through the flight deck entirely to land in the engine rooms or galley below, a mass of twisted, mangled machinery and, presumably, a rather embarrassed pilot looking forward to a not entirely matey chat with the captain whose ship he had just broken. None of the crew members around us remarked on it, though, and I quickly learned that that was because these slam-downs on to the deck were the normal way of going about things here.

Needless to say, it was all quite fantastically manly and rugged. As a fine spray of rain and sea water whipped about us, plane after plane threw itself on to the deck and each was then pounced upon by a team who tended to the immediate needs of this tired and thirsty new arrival. I watched one particular plane as the canopy opened and the pilot's helmeted head surveyed the ship, presumably carrying out last checks and shutdown procedures and getting ready to step out and leave the machine in the hands of its carers on board. As the pilot descended the ladder down the side of the Harrier, something about him caused me to look a little longer than I had at the other pilots making the same descent. And then a little longer again. Something about the design of his flying overalls maybe, or the cut of his jacket. Or his shapely form as he touched down on to the deck. Clearly, this pilot was female and I was, it must be said, quite glad to realise this as my thoughts up to that point would otherwise have been an indication that I might have to consider breaking something a bit tricky to Mindy concerning a forthcoming rather radical lifestyle change.

'Erm, is that pilot, er …?' I screamed over the noise to a crew member standing nearby, eyes shielded by huge, plastic goggles and ears hidden under hard, shiny ear protectors.

'A woman? Yes, she is.' His gaze followed mine to the deck below as the pilot in question retreated into the ship.

'Right, er, of course. Yes, well I knew that. Obviously.' I shouted into the wind. I am sure that the crew member did not pick out the words, but he returned my smile and set off to do whatever his job was on board an aircraft carrier now reunited with its aircraft.

Of course, as a younger man the appearance of a female Harrier pilot would have caused me to raise an eyebrow and possibly even emit a small gasp of astonishment. Clearly, though, as a man of very nearly forty years I could take such a thing in my stride. This is, after all, the twenty-first century and women have been flying combat aircraft for some years now. And rightly so – they are, apparently, rather exceptionally good at it, too. Nevertheless, I had a strong word with myself about not showing the team up and getting remotely giddy about such a thing. To all on board, this pilot would be just one of the many who would pass through the ship in all manner of circumstances. I would, once again, draw upon the lessons I had learned as I made my approach to forty just as these same pilots, including the female one, had made their approaches to the ship, and comport myself with the sense and dignity appropriate to my age and stage in life.

We were invited to dine in the Officers' Mess. We were required to wear formal suits. The pilots would be there and this was a chance to meet up with the other side of this huge floating operation. The event had, thus far, passed off rather well really. I had been seated at a table with some of the pilots, some of the ship's senior officers and, briefly, the captain himself. Also at my table was the female Harrier pilot. I may still have been feeling the effects of the evening spent in the Senior Rates Mess or it may have been that my hearing was still somewhat impaired after the battering it had taken as the jets landed. But, whatever the cause, the fact remains that I was, according to later reports from members of my TV crew, speaking very loudly that evening. I had just asked the pleasant chap sitting next to me, apropos of nothing really, just out of interest you understand, if it was unusual for women to fly Harriers these days. He had told me that, while unusual, it was not at all unheard of. And that these things tend to run in families and be shared among couples. Often a couple will be wedded to one of the armed forces as well as to each other. This lady in question was, in fact, married to a Tornado pilot.

'Bloody hell,' I responded – again, quite loudly according to subsequent reports. Quite a few heads turned to look at me at this point, I am told. 'A Harrier pilot and a Tornado pilot, married, eh?' More heads had turned by now as my voice really was stuck, it seemed, at maximum volume. According to all accounts, though, I managed to find a little more from somewhere and turned it up to '11' to deliver the final part of my statement. 'Well, you wouldn't want to get stuck with the hotel bedroom next to theirs, would you? Can you imagine the racket?' Quite a lot of heads were turned in my direction now, including the one belonging to the Harrier pilot I had just shouted about. The Royal Navy, while managing to enjoy a surprising quality of life in even the most difficult of circumstances – indeed, being specialists at finding fun and being happy even when things are at their toughest – does, nevertheless, have standards of behaviour. And these standards of behaviour take a rather dim view of bawdy or raucous comments at the dinner table in the Officers' Mess and in the presence of the captain. And in the presence of ladies, fighter pilots or otherwise.

The silence that followed was brief, but of such a depth that I feared I might fall into it, screaming soundlessly, and never emerge again. It was the soundman, Grant, who saved me, with a few words chosen, it seemed, almost entirely at random but sufficient all the same to save me from perishing at the bottom of that fathomless silence.

'I thought the noise was incredible, didn't you? I mean, you could really feel it in your chest.' And as Grant thumped his own chest to punctuate his words, the atmosphere relaxed and I slid into silent anonymity on a remote corner of the table. Like a Harrier landing on deck, it seemed that the very last part of my approach to forty would be the part most fraught with peril.